D1045280

WHITE LIES

BLACK COMEDY

including

WHITE
LIES

two plays by

𝖘𝖉

PETER SHAFFER

STEIN AND DAY/*Publishers*/New York

Copyright © 1967 Reath Enterprises

Library of Congress Catalog Card No. 67–25154

All rights reserved

CAUTION: Professionals and amateurs are hereby warned that *Black Comedy* and *White Lies*, being fully protected under the Copyright Laws of the United States of America, the British Commonwealth, including the Dominion of Canada, and all other countries of the Berne and Universal Copyright Conventions, are subject to royalty. All rights, including professional, amateur, motion picture, recitation, lecturing, public reading, radio and television broadcasting, and the rights of translation into foreign languages are strictly reserved. Particular emphasis is laid on the question of readings, permission for which must be secured in writing from the author's agent: Robert Lantz Literary Agency, 111 West 57 Street, New York, N.Y. 10019.

Designed by Bernard Schleifer

Printed in the United States of America

Stein and Day/*Publishers*/7 East 48 Street, New York, N.Y. 10017

Photographs by courtesy of Friedman-Abeles

BY THE SAME AUTHOR

Five Finger Exercise

The Private Ear: The Public Eye

The Royal Hunt of the Sun

Black Comedy was first presented at Chichester, England by the National Theatre on July 27, 1965, and subsequently at The Old Vic Theatre, London, with the following cast:

BRINDSLEY MILLER	Derek Jacobi
CAROL MELKETT	Louise Purnell
MISS FURNIVAL	Doris Hare
COLONEL MELKETT	Graham Crowden
HAROLD GORRINGE	Albert Finney
SCHUPPANZIGH	Paul Curran
CLEA	Maggie Smith
GEORG BAMBERGER	Michael Byrne

Black Comedy and *White Lies* were first presented in New York at the Ethel Barrymore Theater on February 12, 1967 by Alexander Cohen with the following cast:

WHITE LIES

SOPHIE: BARONESS LEMBERG	Geraldine Page
FRANK	Donald Madden
TOM	Michael Crawford

BLACK COMEDY

BRINDSLEY MILLER	Michael Crawford
CAROL MELKETT	Lynn Redgrave
MISS FURNIVAL	Camila Ashland
COLONEL MELKETT	Peter Bull
HAROLD GORRINGE	Donald Madden
SCHUPPANZIGH	Pierre Epstein
CLEA	Geraldine Page
GEORG BAMBERGER	Michael Miller

All three productions were directed by JOHN DEXTER.

WHITE
LIES

For
Paul
with
love

Characters

SOPHIE: BARONESS LEMBERG

FRANK

TOM

PLACE: *The play happens in the Fortune Teller's parlor of* SOPHIE, BARONESS LEMBERG, *on the promenade of a run-down seaside resort on the south coast of England.*

TIME: *The present. Around six o'clock in the evening: mid-September.*

SOPHIE's *Parlor is in fact a seedy living room facing the sea. One side of it is almost entirely occupied by a window, in which is spelled out in cheap gold letters (and in reverse, so that it can be read from outside):* BARONESS LEMBERG, PALMISTE. CLAIRVOYANTE. *And in smaller letters:* CONSULTANT TO ROYALTY. *Through this window you can glimpse a rusting iron balustrade, painted resort-green, and the bleak six o'clock sky of a disastrous English September.*

The entrance is on the other side, and leads into a sort of waiting room, partially visible when the door is open. A second door takes you from the waiting room into the streets; over it is suspended a loud bell to warn SOPHIE *if* SHE *has a client.*

The room is occupied by dusty, broken-down furniture. The most noticeable article of this is the fortune-telling table: an old chilblained Victorian thing, covered with baize and placed centrally on a rotting carpet. On either side of it stands an equally bunioned Victorian chair—and the same swollen decrepitude extends to the sideboard at the right and the little dressing table at the back.

There are two photographs in the room. One, on a wall, is of a huge man's hand and is clearly visible. The other—larger, and far more important to the action—stands on the side table with its back to the audience and, save for the frame, is in-

visible. This is a picture of Vassili, SOPHIE's *friend. It stands as far as possible from the other important friend in her life: Pericles the Parakeet—who is equally invisible inside his wire cage by the window. The* BARONESS' *life in this room alternates between these two poles, the photograph and the cage.*

As the curtain rises, the stage is apparently empty. Presently, however, we hear the sound of singing, issuing from one of the high-backed Victorian chairs facing directly upstage: "A Hard Day's Night" sung in a Germanic accent. Presently a hand lifts up and throws a whole fan of playing cards irritatedly onto the table. SOPHIE *has evidently been playing patience.* SHE *rises wearily and moves over to the window, through which the light comes drear and thick.*

SOPHIE *is a woman of about forty-eight years old. Her appearance is rather neglected; bears the palpable signs of poverty; and is not enhanced by a German fondness for blouses and long woolen skirts. When* SHE *speaks her voice is marked by a marked, but never incomprehensible, German accent, and her delivery is mainly swift and vigorous.*

Now SHE *stares through the window in bleak distress.*

SOPHIE. Look at it. The sea. Like they've poured out ten million cups of tea. No wonder they call it the English Channel. Not one gleam of sunlight in ten days! Not one soul out. Not one miserable holidaymaker walking, jetty to jetty. Nothing but wet sand, rusty iron—and salt on the windows . . . Grinmouth-on-Sea: Fairyland of the South coast! Grinmouth-on-Tea! (*To the photo.*) You hear that, Vassi, I made a joke. (*Sarcastic.*) Oh no, don't laugh. The Germans have no sense of humor, it's well known. Only the Greeks are witty, jaja, I'm sure . . . (*To the cage.*) Perry likes it anyway, don't you? No? . . . Are you sulking too? Well, I

don't blame you. Poor little Pericles. Look, I'll tell your fortune—cheer you up? . . . Ja? . . . "You are to fly away on a
long long journey!" (SHE *laughs*.) . . . Only where would you
go, poor little thing? Down the promenade to the chemist?
Up to the Fish and Chips Shop? . . . One thing is sure,
you'd never find your way home again.

(*Gulls and wind.*)

Beloved God, this silence! You would think someone would
consult me, if only to ask should they kill themselves! . . .
Do you know what I think? Everybody has left town behind
our backs. Just taken a train—the whole population at once,
away to London—and we are left: Sophie—Vassili—and Pericles the Parakeet. The unholy three! . . . Do you realize
there hasn't been an actual human being in this place for
six days? And then it was only Mr. Bowler Hat—if you call
him human! "Mrs. Lemberg, I have to inform you you owe a
million pounds in rent!" Or was it two? Next time he comes
he'll close us: that's for certain. I haven't paid him a penny
since June. (*Irritated.*) Oh, Vassili, what's funny *now*? Do
you never do anything but giggle? Honest, sometimes I don't
understand you at all. Maybe it's specially Greek to laugh
at the serious things of life: if so, I don't appreciate it! I'm
in real difficulties, don't you understand? I owe two months'
rent, and not a client for days. Is that so amusing? . . .
Sometimes I think you're going to stay a child all your life . . .

(SHE *walks away from the photograph, then stops.*)

What's that? . . . How charming! What an exquisite thing
to say! I suppose you think you're talking to one of your
upstart ladies from Athens. Well, let me remind you who I
am. A Lemberg. The Baroness Lemberg. (*Sharply.*) You came
here to learn history, well, so—here's some homework for
you. My family was great under Maria Theresa. What you

had then in your so wonderful Greece were goats. Human
goats, my dear, living on curd milk! All right? . . . (*Exasperated.*) Oh for God's sake now, are you going to sulk?
All right—join Perry. Sulks for the evening: how amusing!
. . . I spend my life with a bird and a child, and I don't
know which is the more boring!

(SHE *sits. Her tone becomes penitent.*)

I'm sorry, Vassi: my tongue runs off with me sometimes.
I know how dreary it is for you in the house. Go out and
see Irina. I tell you what: why don't you invite her here tomorrow for tea? . . . (*Sweetly.*) Ja, of course I mean it! You
are charming together—I like to see you with her, I've told
you. You are so perfect together. So right together. Really.
Right together . . .

(*The bell clashes.* SOPHIE *is startled.*)

Who is it?

(*Silence.*)

Who is it?

(*Silence.*

Speaking through the crack.)

One minute, please. Would you mind waiting in the room
down the corridor? I'll receive you in a moment! . . .

(*Shutting the door.*)

Beloved God, there are two of them! Two whole clients!
I don't believe it. And on a day like this—it's incredible! . . .
That's two whole pounds—think of it. Four if they take the
crystal ball.

(SHE *adjusts her hair, takes her shawl and fan.*)

Well they're going to take the crystal ball whether they like
it or not . . . I only hope I can remember everything. One
gets so rusty! . . . (*To Vassili.*) Oh shut up, you!—that's
not funny . . . Ja, I have news for you. It takes a fraud to

call a fraud: that's what I say! You were a liar in your baby carriage, I'm sure of it! . . . (*Addressing herself to the plants.*) Oh don't droop so—boring middle class plant! . . . Now come on everyone, for God's sake! A little regality around here, please!

(SHE *opens the door.*)

I'm ready now. Come in please, one of you!

(FRANK *enters: a boy of about twenty-five, cold, watchful, ambiguous.* HE *wears a leather jacket.* SOPHIE *is immediately alarmed.*)

FRANK. Are you the witch?

SOPHIE. I am the Baroness Lemberg.

FRANK. Consultant to royalty?

SOPHIE. Exactly.

FRANK. You mean thrones have tottered at the flick of your ace-king-jack?

SOPHIE. Perhaps.

(HE *lounges across the room and looks at the photograph on the wall.*)

FRANK. Whose hand is that?

SOPHIE. A murderer. That is the left hand of Ulf Momsen, the Stockholm Strangler. It has the most remarkable Line of Fate. You can see the suicide in it, quite clearly.

FRANK. You *can?*

SOPHIE. *I* can.

FRANK. I like your slogan outside: "Lemberg Never Lies." Is it true?

SOPHIE. Of course.

FRANK. What a pity.

SOPHIE. I beg your pardon?

FRANK. This place stinks a bit, doesn't it? Bird shit and tinned

[13]

spaghetti. I suppose you eat it to improve your mystic powers. (*Examining the cage.*) Who's this? Your familiar?

SOPHIE. Please?

FRANK. All witches have familiars, don't they? Creepy little animals they share confidences with. I suppose you'd lose all your mystic powers without him, wouldn't you? (*To the bird.*) Hallo, then. What's up with you? Miserable little bugger aren't you? . . . I bet you've heard some nasty predictions in this room, eh?

SOPHIE. Stand away, mister, please. He's a very sensitive bird.

FRANK. That's all right. I'm an expert on sensitive birds.

SOPHIE. (*Sharply.*) I told you, he's sensitive. So please come away from there!

FRANK. What a harsh lady.

SOPHIE. I imagine you want your fortune told. Let me give you my scale of charges. (SHE *hands him a board.*) One pound for cards alone. Thirty shillings for cards and palms. Two pounds for the crystal ball. The ball of course is by far the most profound. It costs just a little more—but then in this world, if one wants the best, one has to pay for it, doesn't one? (SHE *gives him a ravishing smile.*)

FRANK. Yes.

SOPHIE. So which will it be?

FRANK. None.

SOPHIE. I beg your pardon?

FRANK. None.

SOPHIE. Then . . . what do you want?

FRANK. A giggle.

SOPHIE. A giggle?

FRANK. Yeh. We live in dull times. It's our duty to make them gayer, don't you agree? I hope you like jokes yourself.

[14]

SOPHIE. If the situation is amusing, sir, I think I can manage a
—what? A giggle . . .

FRANK. Good. A humorous lady! I'm glad to hear that, Baroness. Because that's what I want to consult you about. That's
what I want to create right here in this room—an amusing
situation.

SOPHIE. Create?

FRANK. Exactly. For him—the boy who's come here with me.
You see, him and me, we have this crazy relationship going,
like, well we kid all the time—have the laugh on each other:
you know. What they call practical jokes. Some people think
it's adolescent. I hope you don't.

SOPHIE. That depends.

FRANK. He's a clever kid—very impressionable. I got him here
to see you by telling him you were one of the most famous
fortune tellers in the western world. Doing a summer season
for her health's sake.

(SHE *lowers her eyes and makes modest noises.*)

His name's Tom, and he's lead singer with our group. We're
called the White Lies. I don't suppose you've ever heard of
us.

SOPHIE. On the contrary, you are singing tonight: . . . (*in the
manner of a clairvoyante*) at the Holiday Camp!

FRANK. (*Impressed.*) How d'you know that?

SOPHIE. (*Laughing.*) I saw it on the poster! You're on the same
bill with the Lettuce Leaves. That's a pity: they're lousy.
However, you have the Serial Numbers to top the bill, and
they are excellent.

FRANK. Well, well, a fan!

SOPHIE. A vulgar word, but true. Are you any good?

FRANK. He's good. A real talent. The girls go mad for him . . .

SOPHIE. And you? Do you sing also?

FRANK. Me? No. I'm their Manager.

SOPHIE. Well!

FRANK. (*Staring at her.*) That's my scene, really. I manage.

SOPHIE. (*Nervous.*) How interesting.

FRANK. It can be. It's why I'm here now—to manage this little scene . . . (HE *smiles at her again.*) When we drove into Grinmouth this afternoon and I saw your sign, I thought to myself immediately: Baroness Lemberg, you're the lady for me. In your mysterious parlor I could stage the best joke ever played. I could get him so brilliantly he'd never forget it.

SOPHIE. (*Coldly.*) Really?

FRANK. With your help, of course. And with someone of your fame—consultant to royalty and all that—I wouldn't expect you to do it for nothing. I'm prepared to offer quite a large fee. I'll do anything for a giggle. I really will. (HE *gives his smile.*)

SOPHIE. (*Interested despite herself.*) What kind of giggle would this be exactly, mister?

FRANK. Well it's sort of a game, really. I'd want you to tell him his past, present, and future.

SOPHIE. Well, that's my profession, after all.

FRANK. I mean precisely. I don't mean to be rude—I'm sure you're fine on your own—but with me you'd be perfect, you see? In this envelope are the main facts of Tom's life—things he's told me over the past year. No one else knows them but me. Some of it's pretty lurid stuff. Unhappy childhood. Coal-mining background. Drunken father who beat him and threw his guitar on the fire. It's all here.

SOPHIE. And are you suggesting I *use* this?

FRANK. Well now listen. Tom's a bit dim but he's not an idiot.

You'll have your work cut out for you to convince him you're genuine. That's where the fun comes in. By the time you've finished telling back to him what's in here, he'll be fish-mouthed.

SOPHIE. Mister, I see no joke in this. It's not funny at all.

(*Pause.*)

FRANK. To be honest, Baroness, this game isn't entirely for laughs. Mainly, but not entirely. I see it as a sort of warning game. Like I'm using it to say something to him. Do you understand? I mean, if you can get Tom to the point when he really believes you have the power to see his whole life, he'll really believe you when you see something a bit nasty in his future. It'll sort of scare him off a bit. Do you see?

SOPHIE. Scare him off what?

FRANK. A girl. I told you I was interested in sensitive birds. (*Staring at her necklace, which* SHE *is fingering.*) What are *they?*

SOPHIE. Greek worry beads.

FRANK. Are you worried?

SOPHIE. Why should I be?

FRANK. Her name's Helen, and she's the girl in our Group. She's got a nice voice—nothing special, but it can carry a tune and won't sour the cream. I've known her for a couple of years, on and off. Mostly *on*, if you follow me. In fact these last eighteen months we've had what I'd call a perfect working relationship.

SOPHIE. It sounds very romantic.

FRANK. (*Lightly.*) It isn't romantic: it works, or did till he came along. Tom the Talent. Then things began to change. Mostly with her. She found she couldn't resist all that shy working class charm. The downcast look—Yorkshire mur-

mur: very trendy . . . And when she looked—he looked. I
don't exactly know what's been going on between them:
nothing much I should think at the moment. She's too timid
and he's too hung up on his loyalty to me, which he damn
well should be by the way. I gave that boy a marvelous bloody
chance. And this is his way of repaying me. He thinks I don't
know, you know. Well, it's time we undeceived him, isn't it.

SOPHIE. You are in love with this girl?

FRANK. That word's rather got rigor mortis round the edges,
hasn't it? (HE *laughs*.) Look: the way we are is the way I like
it. Cool . . . easy . . . nothing strenuous . . . Anyway, if
there's any leaving ever done in my life I do it: do you see?
. . . (*Quietly*.) Can't you leave them alone?

(SHE *stops fiddling with the beads.*

HE *smiles.*)

I suppose that's why they're called worry beads. Because they
worry other people.

(SHE *returns his smile even more uncertainly. A pause.*)

Well, let's get back to my little game, shall we? By this time
you've done his past and present, and as far as he's concerned you're the hottest thing since the Witch of Endor.
Right. Now you move in for the grand finale. I want you to
have a vision, Baroness. A strange, symbolic vision. Let's set
it right . . . (*Slowly*.) You look a little deeper into your
crystal ball and you see pink. Shocking pink. Helen's dressing
gown. Yeh, that's a good touch—very intimate. You see her
wearing it, a pretty blonde girl lying on a bed. Describe the
bed. Brass rails top and bottom, and above it, a picture on
the wall: some droopy tart holding a lily and flopping her
tresses over a stone balcony. It's called Art Nouveau, which
is French for Sentimental Rubbish. Helen loves it of course!
Anyway, use it. Establish the room. *My* room. You'll have

him goggling! Now look deeper. "Good heavens, there's someone else on the bed! Why, it's you, Tom! And what are you doing, my dear? Gracious me, what a passionate creature you are! You're kissing her neck, running your fingers through her blonde hair . . . (*Mockingly.*) Inside that thin frame of yours is a raging animal, isn't there? . . ." (HE *laughs.*) I'd love to be here during that bit. They've never even held hands I shouldn't think.

SOPHIE. Go on, please.

FRANK. (*Carefully.*) Well now you'll have to darken it a bit, won't you? . . . Change the mood. I'd thought of something like this. I hope you like it . . . The door opens. A man stands there. You can't see his face but he's wearing a green corduroy jacket, with black piping round the lapels. That'll get him best, a detail like that. The lovers look up, eyes wide and guilty! Corduroy begins to move towards them. They try to rise, but they're like glued on the bed. Slow motion. Him coming on—them tangled in the sheets—trying to escape. He arrives at the foot of the bed and suddenly—his hand shoots out—like an order!—and what? Why, the girl's whole manner alters at once. She smiles—takes the hand—allows herself to be lifted up, light as a pink feather—high over the brass rails to safety. Our Tom is left alone . . . And now you see scare in the ball! Tom staring at them both. Them staring back, laughing. Yeh. And what's that now in her hands? Something—it looks like a metal can. Yes, a large metal can. She raises it—upends it—begins to pour from it over the sheets. And then, slowly, Corduroy raises his hands too—a matchbox in the air—strikes it—drops a match on to the bed. (*Very quietly.*) Oh look, the orange! Soft fire like orange squirrels running over the bed, over his legs, over his arms, up on to his head . . . his head bursts into flowers! (*Gesturing dream-*

ily.) The whole ball becomes orange—flame whirling, raging inside the crystal, obliterating everything. Then slowly it sinks in. Glass pales from orange to pink, to grey: it clears. And then you see him. Tom the Talent. Still sitting upright on my bed—mouth open, one arm raised—like a salute to death. The only difference is—the whole figure is made of ash. (*Pause*.) Interpret that vision, Baroness. Question it. "Who is this corduroy jacket?" "That's Frank" he'll say. "Well know something, Tom. Frank and that girl are right together. Leave them alone."

SOPHIE. (*Softly*.) "Right together?"

FRANK. "If you come between them, it'll mean disaster for you. Maybe even death."

SOPHIE. "Right together."

FRANK. "Right together." "Belong together." What's it matter? Just so long as you scare him out of his wits.

SOPHIE. For a giggle.

FRANK. Yes, a joke, that's it. We all of us have different senses of humor, Baroness.

SOPHIE. Who am I?

FRANK. What's that?

SOPHIE. Who am I? Some silly gypsy bitch in a caravan you can buy for a couple of pounds?

FRANK. I was thinking of more than that.

SOPHIE. (*Angry*.) Four—five—what's the difference? It's what you think, I can see it: the mad old fake, she'll take anything I offer. Well, mister, let me tell you: you're dealing with a very different kind of lady, I assure you!

FRANK. Oh, come off it!

SOPHIE. (SHE *thrusts her hand at him*.) Look at this! It has held the hand of a Grand Duchess in intimate spiritual communion! It has held Governors—Ministers of Justice—Princes of the Blood!

FRANK. Yes, I see them now—thronging the outer salon!

SOPHIE. Very amusing. Look, mister, I'm not mad, you know, there are no Duchesses out there, I know that. Just crazy spinsters, stinking of moth balls, old red men with gin in their eyes, begging me to predict just one horse race, one football pool, to make them rich for life. Rubbish people, all of them, boring me to death with their second-rate dreams. Nevertheless, I make adjustment. Other years—other tears! I spend my life now casting prophetic pearls before middle class swine. But one thing always: I may hate them, but I do not cheat them. *Lemberg never lies!*

(*Pause.*)

FRANK. (*Quietly.*) Is that how you think of me, Baroness? One of the swine?

SOPHIE. (*Frightened.*) Of course not.

FRANK. I hope not. I really do hope not.

SOPHIE. I merely say . . .

FRANK. (*Interested.*) What do you merely say?

SOPHIE. That if you think I betray my art for a few pounds, you are badly mistaken.

FRANK. Would I be equally mistaken if it was twenty-five pounds?

SOPHIE. Twenty-five?

FRANK. As you said, if you want the best, you've got to pay for it.

SOPHIE. I don't understand. Why don't you just tell him to leave her alone?

FRANK. If I do anything, Baroness, I do it with style. My own style. You do your job right, this'll work a treat.

SOPHIE. He may guess.

FRANK. And even if he does—he'll still get the message. What's

your answer? . . . Look—we've kept him waiting long
enough. Yes or no?

SOPHIE. Disgusting! It's disgusting! . . .

FRANK. Twenty-five quid, dear.

(*Pause.*)

SOPHIE. (*Low.*) All right!

FRANK. A sensible lady. I'll go and fetch him.

SOPHIE. (*Disturbed.*) No—wait!

FRANK. What?

SOPHIE. Give me a minute, please, I must learn this stuff . . .
(SHE *picks up the envelope.*)

FRANK. All right. I'll keep him waiting, tell him how great you
were, reading me. But hurry it up.

SOPHIE. Ja, ja . . . I'll call out when I'm ready.

FRANK. O.K. (HE *goes to the door.*) No tricks now, Baroness.
I would hate you to try keeping that money without earning
it. When he comes out of this room I want to see scare in
his face, like I've never ever seen it.

(HE *goes out.*

SHE *stares after him in horror.*)

SOPHIE. Beloved God! Beloved God, beloved God, beloved God!
. . . (*Shouting at the photo.*) Ja, I know, he's a nut—one
more horror, so what? You've seen them before. The world
is full of perverts. Business is business, for God's sake. And
there's almost half the rent here—just for ten minutes' work!
Anyway, what's it matter? He'll be another horror, just you
see! A little backstreet nothing who wants to be a singer because he can't do a decent day's work! He'll deserve it!
Everyone deserves it! Look, everyone cheats a little, my darling, even your Greek witches. What do you think your famous oracle at Delphi was doing?—one silly cow sitting in a
lot of smoke, saying exactly what she was paid to say! Any-

way I tell you once more and that's the end. It is the duty of the aristocracy to maintain itself, no matter what! Now kindly leave me to study these!

(SHE *sits and writes carefully on her fan.*)

"Born 1945 . . . Coal mines . . . Mother dead. Father drunkard . . . Guitar." Now!

(SHE *tears open the envelope and shows him the money.*)

Look! Do you see? I bet you've never seen so much money in all your life! Think what it means! More Beatle records, more little hats like you were starting the Russian Revolution! And next Sunday, if you are good, a taxi—and not a lousy bus! What do you say? . . . All right, go to her! Always the same threat—the same threat. If that's the best you can manage—then go to her. See if I care!

(SHE *rolls the money, snaps a rubber band over it, and thrusts it inside her blouse. Then* SHE *opens the door.*)

Misters!

(*Returning.*)

Go—go—go—go!

(FRANK *returns with* TOM. HE *is a shy-looking boy of twenty-two, with a thick Cheshire accent.* FRANK *is now very calm, and over-polite.*)

FRANK. This is my friend Tom. Tom, this is the Baroness Lemberg. The greatest fortune teller in the world.

SOPHIE. (*Modestly.*) Please! . . . How do you do?

TOM. Hallo.

FRANK. I've been telling him how incredible you are. I hope you don't mind.

SOPHIE. Such powers as I have, mister, I regard as a gift from the Lord God.

FRANK. Just what I was telling him. It's almost a religious experience, being read by you.

[23]

SOPHIE. I do my best to convey the truth as I see it.

FRANK. And lady, you certainly see it! I was wondering actually if I could stay and watch you read him. I'd be very quiet.

SOPHIE. I'm afraid that's quite out of the question. Your emanations would be very disturbing.

FRANK. Couldn't you just ignore my emanations?

SOPHIE. I appreciate your enthusiasm, mister. People of art are always nourished by enthusiasm. All the same I have a basic rule. One client: one set of emanations.

TOM. Dead right!

FRANK. Very well.

SOPHIE. May I suggest you go for a promenade? When you return in fifteen minutes, you will be refreshed and your friend, I hope, satisfied.

FRANK. Fine. (*To* TOM.) Good luck, then. You're in for a marvelous time, I can tell you. (HE *goes.*)

SOPHIE. So. Sit down, please. (HE *sits.*) Such a flatterer, your friend.

TOM. No, I think he means it. I've never seen him so excited. He's not easily impressed, I can tell you.

SOPHIE. Nor you.

TOM. Me?

SOPHIE. You have disbelieving eyes.

TOM. Oh, yeah?

SOPHIE. (*Quickly.*) You will take the crystal ball of course!

TOM. Will I?

SOPHIE. Of course, my dear. It's more profound. And I can see you deserve the most profound measures.

TOM. Thank you!

SOPHIE. (*Getting the ball.*) You're a musician.

(HE *is startled.*)

Oh don't worry! Remember, I've just read your friend. I presume you are in the Group he manages. It's an easy guess, after all.

(SHE *sets the ball down on the table*.)

There. Just a ball of glass. Except of course that nothing is *just* anything. Give me something you wear, please . . . (HE *starts taking off his overcoat*.) A handkerchief will do. (HE *gives her his handkerchief*.) Thank you. You're very pale. Why?

TOM. No sun, I suppose.

SOPHIE. (*Sitting*.) It's enough, God knows. Every day I look at the sea and hate it all over again. Not once this year have I seen it blue. I think: that's not a sea—it's a gutter between here and France! (SHE *uncovers the ball and puts his handkerchief on it*.) Hang your coat up: you're here for a few minutes, after all.

TOM. (*Rising*.) Thanks.

SOPHIE. All the same I'd say you don't care too much for the sun. You have a winter face.

TOM. Me?

SOPHIE. You like winter best, ja? Rain and storms?

TOM. Could be.

SOPHIE. You're cautious with me. You have no need.

TOM. I'm sorry. Frank said not to say anything at all.

SOPHIE. I think we can discuss the weather without you thinking me a fraud.

TOM. (*Smiling*.) I think so too. You're right. I love days like this. And seaside towns—but only out of season. When no one's there.

SOPHIE. Like here *in* season.

TOM. Oh much worse! I mean, deserted. Dead, dead of winter! . . . I went to Herne Bay last March. It was so cold the rims of your ears felt like they were being gnawed through. The tide was out, and there was snow on the seaweed.

SOPHIE. Snow?

TOM. Yes, it popped when you walked on it. All the sea gulls were sitting in those little shelters that are for people in the summertime. They looked like rows of old convalescents, huddled down in their coat collars.

(SHE *stares at him. Wind, outside the window.*)

SOPHIE. Mister, I do not feel so well this evening. I'm afraid I won't be able to read you.

TOM. You won't?

SOPHIE. I have a headache coming. I feel it. In a minute it will be very painful.

TOM. How do you know?

SOPHIE. (*Loftily.*) Migraine is one of the penalties of divination!

TOM. I'm sorry.

SOPHIE. You'll have to go. You can wait for your friend in the other room.

TOM. Yes. Well . . . good-bye.

SOPHIE. Ja.

(HE *takes his coat and goes to the door.* HE *hesitates.*)

You want something?

TOM. No.

SOPHIE. Er . . . Your handkerchief.

TOM. Oh! Yes!

(HE *comes back to claim it.* SHE *hands it to him.*)

SOPHIE. Can that be only no sun—your paleness?

TOM. What else?

SOPHIE. You think I'm a fake. But somewhere in the back of your head, as you walked here tonight, you were thinking something. Well?

TOM. I suppose what you always think about fortune tellers.

You read stories of people going in for a laugh, coming out
changed for life.

SOPHIE. You want to be changed for life?

TOM. Who doesn't?

SOPHIE. Then sit down again.

TOM. No, I'll be off now. I think I'm a bit mad sometimes:
honest.

SOPHIE. Sit, please.

TOM. No, really—

SOPHIE. (*Sharp.*) Look, mister, what kind of a gentleman are
you? You come here to ask my advice. I settle myself to give
it. Then without a word of respect you turn your back and go!

TOM. You *told* me to go!

SOPHIE. Don't argue with a Baroness! Why do you people have
no breeding?

TOM. I'm sorry—

SOPHIE. Then sit!

(*Bewildered,* TOM *hangs up his coat again.*)

Look, mister. Just for a giggle—you with your paleness—me
with my headache—why don't we explore a little the possi-
bility of changing your life? All right?

TOM. (*Sitting.*) All right.

SOPHIE. I'll tell you a little your past, a little your present: then
your future. (SHE *stares into the ball.*) Mmm. It's very disturbed. There's much confusion . . . 1945. You were born
in 1945?

TOM. (*Surprised.*) Yes!

SOPHIE. It's very ritualistic, the ball. Often first it gives the date
of birth, then the place . . . Ja! Exactly! . . . Ah! I see now
a place. A dirty street. A little narrow house: brown: wet:
working-class. Somewhere in the North, maybe . . . In the

background a huge wheel turning. A coal mine! Ja—a coal village.

(TOM *reacts to this, very startled.*)

I see I'm not too far from the truth. There's no woman in the house. Your mother is dead, ja? . . . Your father still alive. At least I see a man in working clothes—bad face— brutal face—heavy, like a drunk man.

(HE *stares at her, riveted.*)

And what's this now? I see a child. A little pale face—Pale! Eyes frightened. Oh, mister, no! Such a frightened face! . . . He ill-treated you?

(SHE *stares at him.* HE *looks away quickly.*)

Beat you, ja? . . . I must look closer here . . . What's this now? A fire. On it I see something, burning.

TOM. (*Nervously.*) What? . . . What? . . .

SOPHIE. A guitar. Can it be a guitar? . . . What is it? A symbol perhaps of your music talent?

(TOM *rises, terrified.*)

I disturb you, mister?

TOM. You saw *that?* . . .

SOPHIE. Very plain.

TOM. No—it's impossible. It *is!* . . .

SOPHIE. I'm sorry. It was absolutely clear.

TOM. You can't. Just—not! . . . My head—It's here!

SOPHIE. And for me, it's there. You can lock nothing away, my dear. Time that happened once for you, happens now for me . . . Why did he do that? To stop you being a musician? . . . To hurt you? . . .

(TOM, *who has been walking up and down the room, suddenly stops, and stands rigid, struck by something.*)

What is it? Perhaps I should stop now?

TOM. No . . . Go on . . .

SOPHIE. You are upset.

TOM. Doesn't matter . . . It's what I'm paying for, after all.

SOPHIE. I stop.

TOM. (*Urgently.*) No! What else do you see?

(SOPHIE *stares at him: then returns to the ball.*)

SOPHIE. Ah: it's better now. Happiness I think is coming. I see a dot of bright pink, moving toward me. It's a girl. On her head a pink scarf. Very pretty: a blonde girl. You know her?

TOM. Go on.

SOPHIE. Now I see you. She is running to you—you reach out to stop her—but no: she runs right past you. Beloved God!

TOM. What?

SOPHIE. There's someone else. A man. I can't see his face. He wears a green jacket in corduroy. He puts out his hand. She takes it. (*Pause.*) They walk away together—leaving you alone.

TOM. Alone.

SOPHIE. Ja. The alone of alone. More alone than I've ever seen it.

TOM. (*Dead.*) So that's the message. "Alone."

SOPHIE. Does this make sense to you, mister?

TOM. Oh yes. It makes sense. It makes sense . . . (*More to himself.*) What a way to do it!

SOPHIE. To do what, please?

TOM. What a crazy way! To arrange all this—just to let me know! . . . I suppose he set it up as a little joke!

SOPHIE. Who, please?

TOM. No, he could hardly expect you to do it for free. Then it was a few quid on the side.

SOPHIE. What d'you mean?

TOM. Christ, he's crazy! He must be!—

SOPHIE. Young mister, are you suggesting I've been bribed?

TOM. No, I'm not suggesting it. I'm saying it.

SOPHIE. How dare you? How absolutely bloody dare you?

TOM. Because I absolutely know, that's why. There's only one person I've ever told about my childhood—and that's Frank. So, you see.

SOPHIE. My dear, to a professional eye like mine, truth does not have to be told. It is evident.

TOM. I daresay. And what if it isn't the truth?

(*A long pause between them.*)

SOPHIE. I beg your pardon?

TOM. What if it's a zonking great lie . . . Like every word of that story.

(*Pause.*)

SOPHIE. I don't believe it . . .

TOM. It's true.

SOPHIE. Impossible. You say this to discredit me.

TOM. Why should I do that?

SOPHIE. Look, mister, what I see, I see. Lemberg never lies!

TOM. No—but *I do* . . . The bit with the guitar I invented as late as last week.

SOPHIE. You mean your father is not a miner?

TOM. No. He's a very nice accountant, living up in Hoylake.

SOPHIE. And your mother isn't dead?

TOM. Not in the biological sense, no. She likes her game of golf and gives bridge parties every Wednesday.

SOPHIE. But your accent . . .

TOM. (*Letting it drop.*) I'm afraid that's as put on as everything else. I mean, there's no point changing your background if you're going to keep your accent, is there?

SOPHIE. Beloved God!

TOM. Actually, it slips a bit when I'm drunk, but people just think I'm being affected.

[30]

SOPHIE. You mean to say . . . you live your whole life like this. One enormous lie from morning to night?

TOM. I suppose I do.

SOPHIE. Unimaginable!

TOM. Does it worry you?

SOPHIE. Doesn't it worry *you?*

TOM. Sometimes, yes. But not all the time. I've got used to it, I suppose. I regard the whole thing as a sort of . . .

SOPHIE. White lie?

TOM. Yes—very good. A white lie!

SOPHIE. But why? Why? WHY in heaven's name?

TOM. Well, it started as a question of image really. I mean I quickly found out in the world of pop music you've got to be working class to get anywhere. Middle class is right out. No one believes you can sing with the authentic voice of the people if you're the son of an accountant. I mean, sweat's O.K., but taxes turn people off. Do you dig?

SOPHIE. Are you serious?

TOM. Believe me, Baroness: I've worked it out. Look—everyone makes images—*everyone*. It's like no one can look at anyone direct. The way I see it, the whole world's made up of images —images talking at images—that's what makes it all so impossible!

SOPHIE. And do your parents know you've worked it out like this? Disowning them completely?

TOM. No. But they might as well. They've virtually disowned me, after all. Dad calls me "Minstrel Boy" now every time I go home, and mother has a whole bit with her bridge club that I'm in London "studying" music. Studying is a better *image* than singing in clubs. She can *see* herself as the mother of a student. Both of them are talking about themselves, of

course, not me. And I don't blame them. That's what I'm
doing too. And all of us . . .

SOPHIE. What a complicated young mister you are.

TOM. Do you think I'm a bit mad?

SOPHIE. Because you choose to be somebody else? No, that's not
mad. That's not mad. Not entirely.

TOM. I've never told anyone this before. You must have very
special powers.

SOPHIE. Can you really believe that after the way I told your
fortune?

TOM. Well you were pretending then.

SOPHIE. If I were any good, my dear, would I need to pretend?
Oh come: it's me to be embarrassed, not you. It serves me
right for playing silly games. Let's have a drink—what do you
say? Cheer us both up!

TOM. I think it's more than a game to him.

(SHE *rises and goes to the sideboard.*)

SOPHIE. Why?

TOM. Well, he's always pulling gags, but he's never gone this far
before. He can be really marvelous when he wants to. And
then there's another side of him—like this . . . all right, he's
guessed about me and Helen—this is still a pretty weird way
of telling me, isn't it? Is that all he asked you to say to me?
That I was alone?

SOPHIE. (*Avoiding him.*) Mister, please have a drink. I always
take a glass of retsina about this hour in the afternoon. It
tastes like gasoline, but it can be very encouraging.

TOM. Thank you. I think I will.

SOPHIE. My husband would never let me drink when he was
alive. Mind you, he managed a luxury hotel—so he had to be
. . . careful.

TOM. It's so strange his coming here like this. What does he think's going on between Helen and me?

SOPHIE. You feel very strongly about this girl?

TOM. Yes.

SOPHIE. And she about you?

TOM. That's part of it.

(SHE *hands him his drink.*)

SOPHIE. Are you afraid of him?

TOM. I don't know.

SOPHIE. Is she?

TOM. Maybe, I think so, yes.

SOPHIE. Well, that makes three of us.

TOM. You don't know what it can be like sometimes in that house.

SOPHIE. You all three live together?

TOM. Yes. Me upstairs, them down. I wake up every morning thinking of her in his bed. When I come downstairs, he lies there smiling at me.

SOPHIE. Why don't you leave?

TOM. I can't.

SOPHIE. Why not?

TOM. I can't. Isn't it incredible? And every morning I get up and play that part: the coal miner's son frying up breakfast for three! And avoiding her eyes—her great green eyes.

SOPHIE. You mean you haven't even told her the truth?

TOM. Why should I? The real me, as they say, isn't a wow with women. Look! Truth's the last thing she wants. She's "in love"—that's what she calls it! She's in love with a working class boy—even though he doesn't exist. And I'm in love with feelings I see in her eyes—and I know they don't exist. They're only what I read into them. I tell you that's what it's all about—images making noises at images: love!—love!—

love!—love!—(*Pause.*) Love. God, you should see those
eyes . . .

SOPHIE. Ja?

TOM. They're amazing! Like you said, the alone of alone. Well,
these are the green of green.

SOPHIE. Eyes. It's always the eyes.

TOM. I don't know why I'm telling you all this.

SOPHIE. Green or black, it's always the same.

(SHE *rises and moves slowly to the photograph.*)

TOM. I can stretch out quite still for hours, and imagine I'm
lying at the bottom of her eyes.

SOPHIE. With me it was black. Immense black, like the olives.

TOM. Like lying on the bottom of the sea, staring up . . .

SOPHIE. (*Gazing at the photograph.*) He said to me once: "A
Greek proverb for you, Sophie. 'Black eyes are the olives at
the feast of love.'" (*Looking at the photograph.*) He made
it up, of course.

TOM. Who?

SOPHIE. Someone who was lied to.

TOM. He's got a marvelous face.

SOPHIE. Oh yes, white—quite white—with eyes stuck in it so
huge. Like an icon of honesty. I remember the first time I
saw him I thought: "Beloved God, he's dying!" He was paler
even than you. He stood on my doorstep with a little suitcase
in his hand, full of white shirts and a history of the Tudor
kings. He was so polite and thin—like a breathing match-
stick—like you—and he bowed so formal. "My name is
Vassili. I am a student from Greece. Do you have a room,
please? I regret I cannot pay more than three pounds."

TOM. When was this?

SOPHIE. Five years ago. I was a landlady then in Notting Hill.
My husband had died penniless: I had to do something be-

sides tell fortunes. Oh well—other years, other tears! . . .
He was twenty-six years old, but still exactly like a child.
Everything he felt, he gave you, like a present—*shoved* at
you, a joy now, another joy, all day. He used to come into
my room in the evening to watch the television. Always so
neat and careful. "Excuse me, is there rock and roll entertainment tonight?" Now *there* was a fan! He taught me
everything: what groups were good, what lousy, Top Ten,
Pick of the Pops! Secretly I liked it, but it was vulgar to
admit to. After all, I was the Baroness Lemberg. His own
family was just middle class. They sent him what they could,
but it wasn't much. In a while I stopped asking him for rent
. . . and he spent the money instead on pink sweets, yellow
beads, tributes to his lady. He lived for dancing and history!
He was absolutely intoxicated by history! And because I was
an aristocrat, you see, I was supposed to know all about it.
Every Sunday we went on a bus—up to Windsor Castle,
down to St. Paul's Cathedral. And what he never knew was
that every Saturday night I would sit up, secretly memoriz-
ing the facts—then speaking them next day, almost yawning,
because tourism, after all, is a little common, my dear . . .
Typically I never looked at the buildings themselves. Only
their reflections in his eyes. So one bright spring day, I
saw St. Paul's—two tiny little cathedrals swimming in salt
water—and I leaned forward and kissed them, and called him
"Mein Liebe" for the first time.

(*Pause.*)

Can it be you have powers for me too—to make me say
things? . . .

TOM. Go on.

SOPHIE. Well . . . all along there was a fiancée. Her name was
Irina—a slouchy little thing, living with her parents in Lon-

don. She had been chosen for him by the two fathers, who were best friends. Do you know they still do things like that in Greece? He was allowed to take her for walks in the afternoon, but nothing more for two years, till he had finished his studies and could marry. Well, over the months, just because he was forbidden to touch her, he started to whine. "Oh Sophie, I need her so bad. Help me, help me!" And I—because it was so vulgar, you see, to show jealousy —I said to him—

TOM. "Invite her home."

SOPHIE. (*Surprised.*) Ja! . . . "Secretly to your room, in the afternoon. If there are any questions, I shall have been chaperone."

TOM. And she came, of course.

SOPHIE. Every week!

TOM. And you?

SOPHIE. I served them tea . . . into their room with my little tray.

(SHE *picks up the photograph and bears it like a tray over to the table.*)

"Hello, Irina: How are you? How well you look! How's your good father?" And underneath, the *hate!* I, who had never felt hate in my life before, *wasted* its first flood on her; a little *nothing* who never harmed me! Oh, that hate. Burning me so I would cry out to the wallpaper on the stairs—and then into them immediately—smiling, holding out chocolate biscuits. "Oh, Vassili, don't grab them like that. It's so rude at a lady's tea table!"

(SHE *throws the photograph down onto the table.*)

I was you—frying your breakfasts!

TOM. Yes!

SOPHIE. Oh, mister, what pain comes when you start protecting white lies!

(*The lights spring on outside, red and blue.*
SHE *moves toward the window, talking.*)

Dishonest pain. Pain not earned. Pain like an escape from real pain . . . You know the terrible thing? Even now part of me wishes him unhappy, wherever he is, back in Greece, gulping down ice cream in some café, a bright icon with a child's sweet tooth. But then part of me wished *me* unhappy, and who can explain *that*? Always it escapes me. Though now and then, staring here across the water, I think I see the pattern. Then no. Like wrinkles on the skin of the sea, a cold wind rushes up and it dissolves.

(SHE *stares out of the window.*)

TOM. What happened?

SOPHIE. One day he brought me a present. Him—in his little cage. He said: "Here, Sophie, this is Pericles. In Greece he is known as the bird of truth. No one must ever lie in his presence!" He made that up too—*naturally!* "What do you mean," I say to Vassi, "no one must lie?" He sits down giggling. "Sophie, I was talking to Miss Steinberg, that friend who knew you in Germany before the war. She says you were not a Baroness at all. You were a Jewish girl from a poor family: a refugee who married a horrid Englishman who kept a pub. Not a grand hotel, like you said: a pub. And you were not a manageress in a great office. You were only a barmaid."

TOM. He made that up too?

(*Pause.*)

SOPHIE. No, he didn't . . . (*Pause.*) No.

TOM. I see.

SOPHIE. So now standing there, I am ice all over. "Darling," I say, very concerned, "it is time we talked. The two years here are almost up. Our relationship is not fair to Irina. You must think of your marriage." He smiles back—giving me his present, so happy! "I *have* thought, Sophie, and I tell you I do not wish to marry her. I cannot love someone chosen for me by my father." And now it comes! The Baroness speaks for the last time! (*Cooing.*) "That's nonsense, Vassili. You are both young. You are both Greek. You are right together. If you wish to make me happy—*marry her!*"

TOM. No!

SOPHIE. Right together. Very, very right together!

TOM. But why?

SOPHIE. Because it was in his *face*—don't you see?—*I saw it!*

TOM. Saw?

SOPHIE. *Love!* . . . Not despising! Not anger with me! Just love, for me!—smiling in those black eyes. Now we were equal! . . . Now he could *know* me!

(*Pause.*)

Intolerable.

TOM. (*Understanding.*) Yes.

(TOM *gets up, disturbed. There is a long pause.*)

SOPHIE. You asked for the crystal ball.

TOM. I didn't, actually . . . But never mind. (HE *gives her a smile.*)

SOPHIE. Intolerable . . . And for you too? . . . Are you just afraid of seeming middle class? . . . I hope so. You want advice from the witch by the sea? Dare to be known. Dare to love yourself . . . so much. Go to your girl now. Tell her all your lies. She will laugh, I promise you.

TOM. And Frank? Will he laugh too?

SOPHIE. What does that matter? You've never really been afraid of him. Only of yourself. Do you see?

[38]

TOM. Yes, maybe! But still—

SOPHIE. What? Still what?

TOM. I owe him everything. When he found me singing in a Chelsea pub, I didn't have a penny to my name. He founded the group . . . he set me up . . . What kind of thanks is it to steal his girl?

SOPHIE. Thanks?!

TOM. Yes—thanks! Is that so funny?

SOPHIE. (*Slowly.*) Mister, do you want to know what your friend really wanted me to see for you in that crystal ball? Him and your girl burning to ashes. His word—ashes . . .

(*Pause.* HE *looks at her in horror.*)

I'm sorry.

TOM. He said that?—You wouldn't lie. Not about this?—

(*The bell sounds outside. Both glance at it mutely.*)

SOPHIE. No, not to you. (*Urgent and low.*) Go to her now, before the concert, take a deep breath—and tell her everything. I'll deal with him.

TOM. How?

SOPHIE. Just go!

(SHE *propels him to the door.*)

I said before you had disbelieving eyes. It's not true. There is still a little hope in them. Don't let it fade out, mister. Like the sky into the sea. All gray.

TOM. Good-bye, Baroness.

SOPHIE. Sophie.

TOM. Sophie.

(*Suddenly* SHE *kisses him on the cheek. They contemplate each other for a second. Then he opens the door.* FRANK *stands on the other side of it.* TOM *brushes by him and out into the night.* FRANK *lounges into the room, shutting the door.*)

FRANK. Tom: It worked, didn't it? What happened, then?

SOPHIE. I read his fortune.

FRANK. (*Excitedly.*) I bet you did! Come on now—give me every detail, right from the beginning. Don't leave anything out!

SOPHIE. Mister, I'm afraid things have not gone quite as planned.

FRANK. What d'you mean?

SOPHIE. Your friend is more complicated than you think.

FRANK. Why? What happened?

SOPHIE. I don't know.

FRANK. Meaning?

SOPHIE. It grew dark. The lights came on.

FRANK. (*Suddenly hard.*) Look, Baroness, I'm in no mood for games. Where was he off to in such a hurry?

SOPHIE. (*Scared.*) Mister, would you like a drink? Look, maybe I tell your fortune . . . for free!

FRANK. Where was he going, Baroness?

SOPHIE. To his concert, naturally!

FRANK. I don't think so . . . You're lying, aren't you?

SOPHIE. No.

FRANK. Oh yes, you're lying . . . There's cheat in this room. I can smell it. It's hanging in the air like smoke . . . Lady, you cheated me.

SOPHIE. No! I did exactly what you said. I earned my money!

FRANK. (*Disbelieving.*) Lady, you cheated me! . . . He's gone off to—tell Helen, hasn't he? To Helen about all this.

SOPHIE. Of course not.

FRANK. To show me up in front of her—to show me up—to show me up . . . (*Violently.*) You cheating old cow!!!

SOPHIE. Cheat? *Me*—cheat? Me! After what you asked me to do!
. . . Fantastic! . . . (*Furious.*) Listen, Mister—Mr. Cool

and Easy—Mr. Giggle—nobody ever leaves you, do they? Well, news for you! Bloody marvelous news for you. They do—and they will! Tonight! (*Pause.*) You've lost her. But then did you ever really have her?

FRANK. (*Quietly.*) Well, well, well. Who'd have guessed it? Here I was thinking Lemberg may be a bore, but inside that frumpy old bag is a real witch—and all the time she's only a provincial pocket book psychologist. Come on now. Give me back the money.

SOPHIE. No.

FRANK. Come on now. There's a good girl. No witch—no fee. It's fair, you know.

SOPHIE. No!

FRANK. (*Dangerous.*) Hand it over, Baroness.

SOPHIE. No. I need it! I have my rent!

(FRANK *walks deliberately to the cage, reaches in and takes out the bird.*)

FRANK. Last chance, dear. Or no witch—no familiar.

(*Silence. Then:*)

SOPHIE. (*Shouting.*) No!!

(FRANK *looks at her, then opens the window and throws the bird out into the wind.* SOPHIE *shrieks.* THEY *face each other.*)

FRANK. A bird for a bird.

(*A pause.*)

SOPHIE. (*Icy.*) I regret you do not frighten me, sir. Not one hour ago in this room I told Pericles that he would be going on a long, long journey! Perhaps I am not so much a fake, after all.

FRANK. (*Ironically.*) Very brave, Baroness. Very brave and gallant. (*Hard.*) Now—the money.

SOPHIE. I am not a Baroness, mister. My name is Sophie Harburg. And maybe I am not a witch of Endor, but I can still read you. For free.

(SHE *sits, slowly, looking at him.*)

You want your money? Very well.

(SHE *extracts the money from her blouse, takes off the rubber band, and proceeds to deal out the notes onto the table in front of him as if they were cards.*)

Five of pounds: card of cruelty. Five of pounds: card of vanity. Five of pounds: card of stupidity. Five of pounds: card of fantasy. Five of pounds:—card of a loveless life. It's all in the cards, mister.

(HE *stares at her. Then with a swift gesture, sweeps up the notes and leaves the parlor, shutting the door hard behind him. Left alone,* SOPHIE *sits a moment, then reaches out for the photograph lying on the table.*

To Vassili.)

Harburg never lies.

(SHE *drops the photograph gently on the floor, discarding it.*)

Never.

(SHE *stares out at the gathering evening.*)

CURTAIN

IN MEMORY OF
Jerry Weinstein
WHO LAUGHED

Characters

BRINDSLEY MILLER: *A young sculptor (mid-twenties), intelligent and attractive, but nervous and uncertain of himself.*

CAROL MELKETT: *His fiancée. A young debutante; very pretty, very spoiled; very silly. Her sound is that unmistakable, terrifying deb quack.*

MISS FURNIVAL: *A middle-aged spinster. Prissy; and refined. Clad in the blouse and sack skirt of her gentility, her hair in a bun, her voice in a bun, she reveals only the repressed gestures of the middle-class spinster—until alcohol undoes her.*

COLONEL MELKETT: CAROL's *commanding father. Brisk, barky, yet given to sudden vocal calms which suggest a deep and alarming instability. It is not only the constant darkness which gives him his look of wide-eyed suspicion.*

HAROLD GORRINGE: *The camp owner of an antique-china shop, and* BRINDSLEY's *neighbor,* HAROLD *comes from the North of England. His friendship is highly conditional and possessive: sooner or later, payment for it will be asked. A specialist in emotional blackmail, he can become hysterical when slighted, or (as inevitably happens) rejected. He is older than* BRINDSLEY *by several years.*

SCHUPPANZIGH: *A middle-class German refugee, chubby, cultivated, and effervescent. He is an entirely happy man, delighted to be in England, even if this means being employed full time by the London Electricity Board.*

CLEA: BRINDSLEY's *ex-mistress. Mid-twenties; dazzling, emo-*

tional, bright and mischievous. The challenge to her to create a dramatic situation out of the darkness is ultimately irresistible.

GEORG BAMBERGER: *An elderly millionaire art collector, easily identifiable as such.*

THE SET: *The action of the play takes place in* BRINDSLEY's *apartment in South Kensington, London. This forms the ground floor of a large house now divided into flats.* HAROLD GORRINGE *lives opposite;* MISS FURNIVAL *lives above.*

There are four ways out of the room. A door at the left, up-stage, leads directly across the passage to HAROLD's *room. The door to this, with its mat laid tidily outside, can clearly be seen. A curtain, upstage center, screens* BRINDSLEY's *studio: when it is parted we glimpse samples of his work in metal. To the right of this an open stair shoots steeply up to his bedroom above, reached through a door at the top. To the left, downstage, a trap in the floor leads down to the cellar.*

It is a gay room, when we finally see it, full of color and space and new shapes. It is littered with marvelous objects—mobiles, mannikins, toys, and dotty bric-a-brac—the happy paraphernalia of a free and imaginative mind. The total effect is of chaos tidied in honor of an occasion, and of a temporary elegance created by the furniture borrowed from HAROLD GOR-RINGE *and arranged to its best advantage.*

This consists of three elegant Regency chairs in gold leaf; a Regency chaise-longue to match; a small Queen Anne table bearing a fine opaline lamp, with a silk shade; a Wedgwood bowl in black basalt; a good Coalport vase containing summer flowers; and a fine porcelain Buddha.

The only things which actually belong to BRINDSLEY *are a cheap square table bearing the drinks; an equally cheap round*

table in the middle of the room, shrouded by a cloth and deco-
rated with the Wedgwood bowl; a low stool downstage center,
improved by the Buddha; a record player; and his own artistic
creations. These are largely assumed to be in the studio await-
ing inspection; but one of them is visible in this room. On the
dais stands a bizarre iron sculpture dominated by two long
detachable metal prongs, and hung with metal pieces which
jangle loudly if touched. On the wall hang paintings, some of
them presumably by CLEA. *All are non-figurative: colorful geo-*
metric designs, splashes, splodges and splats of color; whirls
and whorls and wiggles—all testifying more to a delight in
handling paint than to an ability to achieve very much with it.

THE TIME: *9:30 on a Sunday night.*

THE LIGHT: *On the few occasions when a lighter is lit,*
matches are struck or a torch is put on, the light on stage
merely gets dimmer. When these objects are extinguished, the
stage immediately grows brighter.

COMPLETE DARKNESS.

Two voices are heard: BRINDSLEY *and* CAROL. THEY *must give*
the impression of two people walking round a room with ab-
solute confidence, as if in the light. We hear sounds as of furni-
ture being moved. A chair is dumped down.

BRINDSLEY. There! How do you think the room looks?
CAROL. (*Quacking.*) Fabulous! I wish you could always have it
  like this. That lamp looks divine there. And those chairs are
  just the right color. I told you green would look well in here.
BRINDSLEY. Suppose Harold comes back?
CAROL. He is not coming back till tomorrow morning.

  (BRINDSLEY *paces nervously.*)

BRINDSLEY. I know. But suppose he comes tonight? He's mad about his antiques. What do you think he'll say if he goes into his room and finds out we've stolen them?

CAROL. Don't dramatize. We haven't stolen all his furniture. Just three chairs, the sofa, that table, the lamp, the bowl, and the vase of flowers, that's all.

BRINDSLEY. And the Buddha. That's more valuable than anything. Look at it.

CAROL. Oh, do stop worrying, darling.

BRINDSLEY. Well, you don't know Harold. He won't even let anyone touch his antiques.

CAROL. Look, we'll put everything back as soon as Mr. Bamberger leaves. Now stop being dreary.

BRINDSLEY. Well, frankly, I don't think we should have done it. I mean—*anyway*, Harold or no.

CAROL. Why not, for heaven's sake? The room looks divine now. Just look at it!

BRINDSLEY. Darling, Georg Bamberger's a multi-millionaire. He's lived all his life against this sort of furniture. Our few stolen bits aren't going to impress him. He's coming to see the work of an unknown sculptor. If you ask me, it would look much better to him if he found me exactly as I really am: a poor artist. It might touch his heart.

CAROL. It might—but it certainly won't impress Daddy. Remember, he's coming too.

BRINDSLEY. As if I could forget! Why you had to invite your monster father tonight, I can't think!

CAROL. Oh, not again!

BRINDSLEY. Well, it's too bloody much. If he's going to be persuaded I'm a fit husband for you, just by watching a famous collector buy some of my work, he doesn't deserve to have me as a son-in-law!

[50]

CAROL. He just wants some proof you can earn your own living.

BRINDSLEY. And what if Bamberger *doesn't* like my work?

CAROL. He will, darling. Just stop worrying.

BRINDSLEY. I can't. Get me a whiskey.

(SHE *does. We hear her steps, and a glass clink against a bottle—then the sound of a soda syphon.*)

I've got a foreboding. It's all going to be a disaster. An A-one, copper-bottomed, twenty-four-carat disaster.

CAROL. Look, darling, you know what they say. Faint heart never won fair ladypegs!

BRINDSLEY. How true.

CAROL. The trouble with you is you're what Daddy calls a Determined Defeatist.

BRINDSLEY. The more I hear about your Daddy, the more I hate him. I loathe military men anyway . . . and in any case, he's bound to hate me.

CAROL. Why?

BRINDSLEY. Because I'm a complete physical coward. He'll smell it on my breath.

CAROL. Look, darling, all you've got to do is stand up to him. Daddy's only a bully when he thinks people are afraid of him.

BRINDSLEY. Well, I am.

CAROL. You haven't even met him.

BRINDSLEY. That doesn't make any difference.

CAROL. Don't be ridiculous. (*Hands him a drink.*) Here.

BRINDSLEY. Thanks.

CAROL. What can he do? To you?

BRINDSLEY. For one thing, he can refuse to let me marry you.

CAROL. Ah, that's sweetipegs.

(THEY *embrace.*)

BRINDSLEY. I like you in yellow. It brings out your hair.

CAROL. Straighten your tie. You look sloppy.

BRINDSLEY. Well, you look divine.

CAROL. Really?

BRINDSLEY. I mean it. I've never seen you look so lovely.

CAROL. Tell me, Brin, have there been many before me?

BRINDSLEY. Thousands.

CAROL. Seriously!

BRINDSLEY. Seriously—none.

CAROL. What about that girl in the photo?

BRINDSLEY. She lasted about three months.

CAROL. When?

BRINDSLEY. Two years ago.

CAROL. What was her name?

BRINDSLEY. Clea.

CAROL. What was she like?

BRINDSLEY. She was a painter. Very honest. Very clever. And just about as cozy as a steel razor blade.

CAROL. When was the last time you saw her?

BRINDSLEY. (*Evasively.*) I told you . . . two years ago.

CAROL. Well, why did you still have her photo in your bedroom drawer?

BRINDSLEY. It was just there. That's all. Give me a kiss . . . (*Pause.*) No one in the world kisses like you.

CAROL. (*Murmuring.*) Tell me something . . . did you like it better with her—or me?

BRINDSLEY. Like what?

CAROL. Sexipegs.

BRINDSLEY. Look, people will be here in a minute. Put a record on. It had better be something for your father. What does he like?

CAROL. (*Crossing to the record player.*) He doesn't like anything except military marches.

[52]

BRINDSLEY. I might have guessed . . . Wait—I think I've got some! That last record on the shelf. The òrange cover. It's called "Marching and Murdering with Sousa," or something.

CAROL. This one?

BRINDSLEY. That's it.

CAROL. (*Getting it.*) "The Band of the Coldstream Guards."

BRINDSLEY. Ideal. Put it on.

CAROL. How d'you switch on?

BRINDSLEY. The last knob on the left. That's it . . . Let us pray! Oh God, let this evening go all right! Let Mr. Bamberger like my sculpture and buy some! Let Carol's monster father like me! And let my neighbor Harold Gorringe never find out that we borrowed his precious furniture behind his back! Amen.

(*A Sousa march; loud. Hardly has it begun, however, when it runs down—as if there is a failure of electricity.*

BRILLIANT LIGHT FLOODS THE STAGE. THE REST OF THE PLAY, SAVE FOR THE TIMES WHEN MATCHES ARE STRUCK, OR FOR THE SCENE WITH SCHUPPANZIGH, IS ACTED IN THIS LIGHT, BUT AS IF IN PITCH DARKNESS.

THEY *freeze:* CAROL *by the end of the sofa;* BRINDSLEY *by the drinks table. The* GIRL's *dress is a silk flag of chic wrapped round her greyhound's body. The* BOY's *look is equally cool: narrow, contained, and sexy. Throughout the evening, as things slide into disaster for him, his crisp, detached shape degenerates progressively into sweat and rumple—just as the elegance of his room gives way relentlessly to its usual near-slum appearance. For the place, as for its owner, the evening is a progress through disintegration.*)

God! We've blown a fuse!

(*The structure and appearance of* BRINDSLEY's *room is described in the note at the beginning of the play.*)

CAROL. *Oh no!*

BRINDSLEY. It must be. (HE *blunders to the light switch, feeling ahead of him, trying to part the darkness with his hands. Finding the switch,* HE *flicks it on and off.*)

CAROL. It is!

BRINDSLEY. Oh no!

CAROL. Or a power cut. Where's the box?

BRINDSLEY. In the hall.

CAROL. Have you any candles?

BRINDSLEY. No. Damn!

CAROL. Where are the matches?

BRINDSLEY. They should be on the drinks table. (*Feeling round the bottles.*) No. Try on the record player.

(THEY *both start groping about the room, feeling for matches.*)

Damn, damn, damn, damn, damn, damn!

(CAROL *sets a maraca rattling off the record player.*)

CAROL. There! (*Finding it.*) No . . .

(*The telephone rings.*)

BRINDSLEY. Would you believe it?!

(HE *blunders his way toward the sound of the bell. Just in time* HE *remembers the central table—and stops himself colliding into it with a smile of self-congratulation.*)

All right: I'm coming!

(*Instead* HE *trips over the dais, and goes sprawling—knocking the phone onto the floor.* HE *has to grope for it on his knees, hauling the receiver back to him by the wire. Into receiver.*)

Hallo? . . . (*In sudden horror.*) Hallo! . . . No, no, no, no— I'm fine, just fine! . . . You? . . . (*His hand over the receiver: to* CAROL.) Darling—look in the bedroom, will you?

CAROL. I haven't finished in here yet.

BRINDSLEY. Well, I've just remembered there's some fuse wire in the bedroom. In that drawer where you found the photograph. Go and get it, will you?

CAROL. I don't think there is. I didn't see any there.

BRINDSLEY. (*Snapping.*) Don't argue. Just look!

CAROL. All right. Keep your hairpiece on.

(*During the following* SHE *gropes her way cautiously up the stairs—head down, arms up the banisters, silken bottom thrust out with the effort.*)

BRINDSLEY. (*Controlling himself.*) I'm sorry. I just know it's there, that's all. You must have missed it.

CAROL. What about the matches?

BRINDSLEY. We'll have to mend it in the dark, that's all. Please hurry, dear.

CAROL. (*Climbing.*) Oh God, how dreary!

BRINDSLEY. (*Taking his hand off the receiver and listening to hear* CAROL *go.*) Hallo? . . . Well, well, well, well! How are you? Good. That's just fine. Fine, fine! . . . Stop saying what?

(CAROL *reaches the top of the stairs—and from force of habit pulls down her skirt before groping her way into the bedroom.*)

BRINDSLEY. (*Hand still over the receiver.*) Carol? . . . Darling? . . .

(*Satisfied* SHE *has gone; in a rush into the telephone, his voice low.*)

Clea! What are you doing here? I thought you were in Finland . . . But you've hardly been gone six weeks . . . Where are you speaking from? . . . The Air Terminal? . . . Well, no, that's not a good idea tonight. I'm terribly busy, and I'm afraid I just can't get out of it. It's business.

CAROL. (*Calling from the bedroom door, above.*) There's nothing there except your dreary socks. I told you.

BRINDSLEY. (*Calling back.*) Well, try the other drawers . . .
(HE *rises as* HE *speaks, turning so that the wire wraps itself around his legs.*
CAROL *returns to her search.*
Low and rapid, into phone.)
Look: I can't talk now. Can I call you tomorrow? Where will you be? . . . Look, I told you *no*, Clea. Not tonight. I know it's just around the corner, that's not the point. You can't come round . . . Look, the situation's changed. Something's happened this past month—

CAROL. (*Off.*) I can't see anything. Brin, *please!*—

BRINDSLEY. Clea, I've got to go . . . Look, I can't discuss it over the phone . . . Has it got to do with what? Yes, of course it has. I mean you can't expect things to stay frozen, can you?

CAROL. (*Emerging from the bedroom.*) There's nothing here. Haven't we any matches at all?

BRINDSLEY. Oh stop wailing! (*Into phone.*) No, not you. I'll call you tomorrow. Good-bye.
(HE *hangs up sharply—but fails to find the rest of the telephone so that* HE *bangs the receiver hard on the table first. Then* HE *has to disentangle himself from the wire. Already* BRINDSLEY *is beginning to be fussed.*)

CAROL. (*Descending.*) Who was that?

BRINDSLEY. Just a chum. Did you find the wire?

CAROL. I can't find anything in this. We've *got* to get some matches!—

BRINDSLEY. I'll try the pub. Perhaps they'll have some candles as well.

(*Little screams are heard approaching from above. It is* MISS FURNIVAL *groping her way down in a panic.*)

MISS FURNIVAL. (*Squealing.*) Help! Help! . . . Oh please some-one help me!

BRINDSLEY. (*Calling out.*) Is that you, Miss Furnival?

MISS FURNIVAL. Mr. Miller? . . .

BRINDSLEY. Yes?

MISS FURNIVAL. Mr. Miller!

BRINDSLEY. Yes!

(SHE *gropes her way in.* BRINDSLEY *crosses to find her, but narrowly misses her.*)

MISS FURNIVAL. Oh, thank God, you're there; I'm so frightened!

BRINDSLEY. Why? Have your lights gone too?

MISS FURNIVAL. Yes!

BRINDSLEY. It must be a power cut. (HE *finds her hand and leads her to the chair downstage left.*)

MISS FURNIVAL. I don't think so. The street lights are on in the front. I saw them from the landing.

BRINDSLEY. Then it must be the main switch of the house.

CAROL. Where is that?

(MISS FURNIVAL *gasps at the strange voice.*)

BRINDSLEY. It's in the cellar. It's all sealed up. No one's allowed to touch it but the electricity people.

CAROL. What are we going to do?

BRINDSLEY. Get them—quick!

CAROL. Will they come at this time of night?

BRINDSLEY. They've got to.

(BRINDSLEY *accidentally touches* MISS FURNIVAL'S *breasts.* SHE *gives a little scream.* BRINDSLEY *gropes his way to the phone.*)

Have you by any chance got a match on you, Miss Furnival?

MISS FURNIVAL. I'm afraid I haven't. So improvident of me. And I'm absolutely terrified of the dark.

BRINDSLEY. Darling, this is Miss Furnival, from upstairs. Miss Furnival—Miss Melkett.

MISS FURNIVAL. How do you do?

CAROL. (*Extending her hand into the darkness.*) How do you do?

MISS FURNIVAL. Isn't this frightful?

(BRINDSLEY *picks up the phone and dials* "O".)

CAROL. Perhaps we can put Mr. Bamberger off.

BRINDSLEY. Impossible. He's dining out and coming on here after. He can't be reached.

CAROL. Oh, flip!

BRINDSLEY. (*Sitting on the dais, and speaking into the phone.*) Hallo, Operator, can you give me the London Electricity Board, please? Night Service . . . I'm sure it's in the book, Miss, but I'm afraid I can't see . . . There's no need to apologize. No, I'm not blind!—I just can't see: we've got a fuse . . . No we *haven't* got any matches! (*Desperate.*) Miss, *please*: this is an emergency . . . Thank you! . . . (*To the room.*) London is staffed with imbeciles!

MISS FURNIVAL. Oh, you're so right, Mr. Miller.

BRINDSLEY. (*Rising, frantic: into the phone.*) Miss, I *don't want* the number: I can't dial it! . . . Well, have *you* ever tried to dial a number in the dark? . . . (*Trying to keep control.*) I just want to be connected . . . Thank you. (*To* MISS FURNIVAL.) Miss Furnival, do you by any remote chance have any candles?

MISS FURNIVAL. I'm afraid not, Mr. Miller.

BRINDSLEY. (*Mouthing nastily at her.*) "I'm afraid not, Mr. Miller" . . . (*Briskly, into phone.*) Hallo? Look, I'd like to report a main fuse at Eighteen Scarlatti Gardens. My name is Miller. (*Exasperated.*) Yes, yes! All right! . . . (*Maddened: to the room.*) Hold on! Hold bloody on!

MISS FURNIVAL. If I might suggest—Harold Gorringe opposite might have some candles. He's away for the weekend, but always leaves his key under the mat.

BRINDSLEY. What a good idea. That's just the sort of practical thing he would have. (*To* CAROL.) Here—take this . . . I'll go and see, love.

(HE *hands her the telephone in a fumble—then makes for the door—only to collide smartly with his sculpture.*)
Bugger!

MISS FURNIVAL. Are you all right, Mr. Miller?

BRINDSLEY. I knew it! I bloody knew it. This is going to be the worst night of my life! . . . (HE *collides with the door.*)

CAROL. Don't panic, darling. Just don't panic!

(HE *stumbles out and is seen groping under* HAROLD's *mat for the key.* HE *finds it and enters the room opposite.*)

MISS FURNIVAL. You're so right, Miss Melkett. We must none of us panic.

CAROL. (*On the phone.*) Hallo? Hallo? (*To* MISS FURNIVAL.) This would have to happen tonight. It's just Brindsley's luck.

MISS FURNIVAL. Is it something special tonight then, Miss Melkett?

CAROL. It couldn't be more special if it tried.

MISS FURNIVAL. Oh, dear. May I ask why?

CAROL. Have you ever heard of a German called Georg Bamberger?

MISS FURNIVAL. Indeed, yes. Isn't he the richest man in the world?

CAROL. Yes. (*Into phone.*) Hallo? . . . (*To* MISS FURNIVAL.) Well, he's coming here tonight.

MISS FURNIVAL. Tonight!

CAROL. In about twenty minutes, to be exact. And to make matters worse, he's apparently stone deaf.

MISS FURNIVAL. How extraordinary! May I ask why he's coming?

CAROL. He saw some photos of Brindsley's work and apparently got madly excited about it. His secretary rang up last week and asked if he could come and see it. He's a great collector. Brin would be absolutely *made* if Bamberger bought a piece of his.

MISS FURNIVAL. Oh, how exciting!

CAROL. It's his big break. Or was—till a moment ago.

MISS FURNIVAL. Oh my dear, you *must* get some help. Jiggle that thing.

CAROL. (*Jiggling the phone.*) *Hallo? Hallo?* . . . Perhaps the Bomb's fallen, and everyone's dead.

MISS FURNIVAL. Oh, please don't say things like that—even in levity.

CAROL. (*Someone answers her at last.*) Hallo? Ah! This is Number Eighteen, Scarlatti Gardens. I'm afraid we've had the most dreary fuse. It's what's laughingly known as the Main Switch. We want a *little man* . . . Well, they can't all have flu . . . Oh, please try! It's screamingly urgent . . . Thank you. (SHE *hangs up.*) Sometime this evening, they hope. That's a lot of help.

MISS FURNIVAL. They're not here to help, my dear. In my young days you paid your rates and you got satisfaction. Nowadays you just get some foreigner swearing at you. And if they think you're of the middle class, that only makes it worse.

CAROL. Would you like a drink?

MISS FURNIVAL. I don't drink, thank you. My dear father, being a Baptist minister, strongly disapproved of alcohol.

(A *scuffle is heard amongst milk bottles off, followed by a stifled oath.*)

COLONEL MELKETT. (*Off.*) Damn and blast!! . . . (*Barking.*)
Is there anybody there?

CAROL. (*Calling.*) In here, daddypegs!

COLONEL. Can't you put the light on, dammit? I've almost
knocked meself out on a damn milk bottle.

CAROL. We've got a fuse. Nothing's working.

(COLONEL MELKETT *appears, holding a lighter which evidently
is working—we can see the flame, and of course, the lights
go down a little.*)

MISS FURNIVAL. Oh what a relief! A light!

CAROL. This is my father, Colonel Melkett, Miss Furnival. She's
from upstairs.

COLONEL. Good evening.

MISS FURNIVAL. I'm taking refuge for a moment with Mr.
Miller. I'm not very good in the dark.

COLONEL. When did this happen?

(MISS FURNIVAL, *glad for the light, follows it pathetically
as the* COLONEL *crosses the room.*)

CAROL. Five minutes ago. The main just blew.

COLONEL. And where's this young man of yours?

CAROL. In the flat opposite. He's trying to find candles.

COLONEL. You mean he hasn't got any?

CAROL. No. We can't even find the matches.

COLONEL. I see. No organization. Bad sign!

CAROL. Daddy, please. It could happen to any of us.

COLONEL. Not to me.

(HE *turns to find* MISS FURNIVAL *right behind him and glares
at her balefully. The poor* WOMAN *retreats to the sofa and
sits down.*

COLONEL MELKETT *gets his first sight of* BRINDSLEY's *sculpture.*)

What the hell's that?

CAROL. Some of Brindsley's work.

COLONEL. Is it, by Jove? And how much does that cost?

CAROL. I think he's asking fifty pounds for it.

COLONEL. My God!

CAROL. (*Nervously.*) Do you like the flat, Daddy? He's furnished it very well, hasn't he? I mean it's rich, but not gaudipegs.

COLONEL. Very elegant—good: I can see he's got excellent taste. (*Seeing the Buddha.*) Now that's what I understand by a real work of art—you can see what it's meant to be.

MISS FURNIVAL. Good heavens!

CAROL. What is it?

MISS FURNIVAL. Nothing . . . It's just that Buddha—it so closely resembles the one Harold Gorringe has.

(CAROL *looks panic-stricken.*)

COLONEL. It must have cost a pretty penny, what? He must be quite well off. . . . By Jove—it's got pretty colors. (HE *bends to examine it.*)

CAROL. (*Sotto voce, urgently, to* MISS FURNIVAL.) You know Mr. Gorringe?

MISS FURNIVAL. Oh, very well indeed. We're excellent friends. He has such lovely things . . . (*For the first time* SHE *notices the sofa on which* SHE *is sitting.*) Oh . . .

CAROL. What?

MISS FURNIVAL. This furniture . . . (*Looking about her.*) Surely—?—my goodness!—

CAROL. (*Hastily.*) Daddy, why don't you look in there? It's Brin's studio. There's something I particularly want you to see before he comes back.

COLONEL. What?

CAROL. It—it—er—it's a surprise, go and see.

COLONEL. Very well, Dumpling. Anythin' to oblige. (*To* MISS
  FURNIVAL.) Excuse me.

  (HE *goes off into the studio, taking his lighter with him.
  The light instantly gets brighter on stage.* CAROL *sits beside
  the* SPINSTER *on the sofa, crouching like a conspirator.*)

CAROL. (*Low and urgent.*) Miss Furnival, you're a sport, aren't
  you?

MISS FURNIVAL. I don't know. What is this furniture doing in
  here? It belongs to Harold Gorringe.

CAROL. I know. We've done something absolutely frightful.
  We've stolen all his best pieces and put Brin's horrid old bits
  into *his* room.

MISS FURNIVAL. But why? It's disgraceful!

CAROL. (*Sentimentally.*) Because Brindsley's got nothing, Miss
  Furnival. Nothing at all. He's as poor as a church mouse.
  If Daddy had seen this place as it looks normally, he'd have
  forbidden our marriage on the spot. Mr. Gorringe wasn't
  there to ask—so we just took the chance.

MISS FURNIVAL. If Harold Gorringe knew that anyone had
  touched his furniture or his porcelain, he'd go out of his
  mind! And as for that Buddha—(*Pointing in the wrong direction.*)—it's the most precious piece he owns. It's worth
  hundreds of pounds.

CAROL. Oh, please, Miss Furnival—you won't give us away, will
  you? We're desperate! And it's only for an hour . . . Oh,
  please! *please!*

MISS FURNIVAL. (*Giggling.*) Very well! I won't betray you!

CAROL. Oh, thank you!

MISS FURNIVAL. But it'll have to go back exactly as it was, just
  as soon as Mr. Bamberger and your father leave.

CAROL. I swear! Oh, Miss Furnival, you're an angel! Do have
  a drink. Oh no, you don't. Well, have a bitter lemon.

MISS FURNIVAL. Thank you. That I won't refuse.

(*The* COLONEL *returns, still holding his lighter. The stage darkens a little.*)

COLONEL. Well, they're certainly a surprise. And that's supposed to be sculpture?

CAROL. It's not supposed to be. It is.

COLONEL. They'd make good garden implements. I'd like 'em for turnin' the soil.

(MISS FURNIVAL *giggles.*)

CAROL. That's not very funny, Daddy.

(MISS FURNIVAL *stops giggling.*)

COLONEL. Sorry, Dumpling. Speak as you find.

CAROL. I wish you wouldn't call me Dumpling.

COLONEL. Well, there's no point wastin' this. We may need it!

(HE *snaps off his lighter.*

MISS FURNIVAL *gives her little gasp as the stage brightens.*)

CAROL. Don't be nervous, Miss Furnival. Brin will be here in a minute with the candles.

MISS FURNIVAL. Then I'll leave, of course. I don't want to be in your way.

CAROL. You're not at all. (*Hearing him.*) Brin?—

(BRINDSLEY *comes out of* HAROLD's *room—returns the key under the mat.*)

BRINDSLEY. Hallo?

CAROL. Did you find anything?

BRINDSLEY. (*Coming in.*) You can't find anything in this. If there's candles there, *I* don't know where they are. Did you get the electric people?

CAROL. They said they might send someone around later.

BRINDSLEY. How much later?

CAROL. They don't know.

BRINDSLEY. That's a lot of help. What a lookout! Not a bloody candle in the house. A deaf millionaire to show sculpture to—and your monster father to keep happy. Lovely!

COLONEL. (*Grimly lighting his lighter.*) Good evenin'.

(BRINDSLEY *jumps.*)

CAROL. Brin, this *is* my father—Colonel Melkett.

BRINDSLEY. (*Wildly embarrassed.*) Well, well, well, well, well! . . . (*Panic.*) Good evening, sir. Fancy you being there all the time! I—I'm expecting some dreadful neighbors, some neighbor monsters, monster neighbors, you know . . . They rang up and said they might look round . . . Well, well, well . . .

COLONEL. (*Darkly.*) Well, well.

MISS FURNIVAL. (*Nervously.*) Well, well!

CAROL. (*Brightly.*) Well!

(*The* COLONEL *rises and advances on* BRINDSLEY *who retreats before him across the room.*)

COLONEL. You seem to be in a spot of trouble.

BRINDSLEY. (*With mad nervousness.*) Oh, not really! Just a fuse—nothing really, we have them all the time . . . I mean, it won't be the first fuse I've survived, and I daresay it won't be the last! (HE *gives a wild braying laugh.*)

COLONEL. (*Relentless.*) In the meantime, you've got no matches. Right?

BRINDSLEY. Right.

COLONEL. No candles. Right?

BRINDSLEY. Right.

COLONEL. No basic efficiency, right?

BRINDSLEY. I wouldn't say that, exactly . . .

COLONEL. By basic efficiency, young man, I mean the simple state of being At Attention in life, rather than At Ease. Understand?

BRINDSLEY. Well, I'm certainly not at ease.

[65]

COLONEL. What are you goin' to do about it?

BRINDSLEY. Do?

COLONEL. Don't echo me, sir. I don't like it.

BRINDSLEY. You don't like it. . . . I'm sorry.

COLONEL. Now look you here. This is an emergency. Anyone can see that.

BRINDSLEY. No one can see anything: that's the emergency. (HE *gives his braying laugh again.*)

COLONEL. Spare me your humor, sir, if you don't mind. Let's look at the situation objectively. Right?

BRINDSLEY. Right.

COLONEL. Good. (HE *snaps off the lighter.*) Problem: Darkness. Solution: Light.

BRINDSLEY. Oh very good, sir.

COLONEL. Weapons: Matches: none! Candles: none! What remains?

BRINDSLEY. Search me.

COLONEL. (*Triumphantly.*) Torches. Torches, sir! what?

BRINDSLEY. Or a set of early Christians.

COLONEL. What did you say?

BRINDSLEY. I'm sorry. I think I'm becoming unhinged. Very good. Torches—brilliant.

COLONEL. Routine. Well, where would you find one?

BRINDSLEY. The pub. What time is it?

(*The* COLONEL *lights his lighter, but now not at the first try. The stage light flickers up and down accordingly.*)

COLONEL. Blasted thing. It's beginnin' to go. (HE *consults his watch.*) Quarter to ten. You can just make it, if you hurry.

BRINDSLEY. Thank you, sir. Your clarity of mind has saved the day.

COLONEL. Well, get on with it, man.

BRINDSLEY. Yes, sir! Back in a minute.

(*The* COLONEL *sits in the Regency chair, downstage right.*)

[66]

CAROL. Good luck, darling.

BRINDSLEY. Thank you, my sweet.

(SHE *blows him a kiss.* HE *blows her one back.*)

COLONEL. (*Irritated.*) Stop that at once.

(BRINDSLEY *starts for the door—but as* HE *reaches it,* HAROLD GORRINGE *is heard, off.*)

HAROLD. (*Broad Lancashire accent.*) Hallo? Hallo? Anyone there?

BRINDSLEY. (*Freezing with horror.*) HAROLD!!

HAROLD. Brindsley?

BRINDSLEY. (*Meant for* CAROL.) It's Harold. He's back!

CAROL. Oh no!

BRINDSLEY. THE FURNITURE!!

HAROLD. What's going on here?

(HAROLD *appears.* HE *wears a smart raincoat and carries a weekend suitcase. His hair falls over his brow in a flossy attempt at elegance.*)

BRINDSLEY. Nothing, Harold. Don't go in there—come in here. We've had a fuse. It's dark—it's all over the house.

HAROLD. Have you phoned the electric? (*Reaching out.*)

BRINDSLEY. (*Reaching out and grabbing him.*) Yes. Come in here.

HAROLD. (*Grabbed.*) Ohh! . . . (HE *takes* BRINDSLEY's *hand and enters the room cozily on his arm.*) It's rather cozy in the dark, isn't it?

BRINDSLEY. (*Desperately.*) Yes! I suppose so . . . So you're back from your weekend then . . .

HAROLD. I certainly am, dear. Weekend! Some weekend! It rained the whole bloody time. I feel damp to my knickers.

BRINDSLEY. (*Nervously.*) Well, have a drink and tell us all about it.

HAROLD. Us? (*Disengaging himself.*) Who's here, then?

MISS FURNIVAL. (*Archly.*) I am, Mr. Gorringe.

HAROLD. Ferny?

MISS FURNIVAL. Taking refuge, I'm afraid. You know how I hate the dark.

COLONEL. (*Attempting to light his lighter.*) Blasted thing! . . . (HE *succeeds.*) There we are! (*Raising it to* GORRINGE'S *face, with distaste.*) Who are you?

BRINDSLEY. May I present my neighbor. This is Harold Gorringe—Colonel Melkett.

HAROLD. How do?

COLONEL. How d'ye do?

BRINDSLEY. And this is Miss Carol Melkett, Harold Gorringe.

CAROL. (*Giving him a chilly smile.*) Hallo! . . .

(HAROLD *nods coldly.*)

BRINDSLEY. Here, let me take your raincoat, Harold.

(HE *is wearing a tight, modish, gray suit and a brilliant, strawberry shirt.*)

HAROLD. (*Taking it off and handing it to him.*) Be careful, it's sopping wet.

(*Adroitly,* BRINDSLEY *drops the coat over the Wedgwood bowl on the table.*)

COLONEL. You got no candles, I suppose?

HAROLD. Would you believe it, Colonel, but I haven't? Silly me!

(BRINDSLEY *crosses and blows out the* COLONEL'S *lighter, just as* HAROLD *begins to look round the room. The stage brightens.*)

COLONEL. What the devil did you do that for?

BRINDSLEY. I'm saving your wick, Colonel. You may need it later and it's failing fast.

(*The* COLONEL *gives him a suspicious look.* BRINDSLEY *moves quickly back, takes up the coat and drops it over the right end of the sofa, to conceal as much of it as possible.*)

[68]

HAROLD. It's all right. I've got some matches.

CAROL. (*Alarmed.*) Matches!

HAROLD. Here we are! I hope I've got the right end. (HE *strikes one.*)

(BRINDSLEY *immediately blows it out from behind, then moves swiftly to hide the Wedgwood bowl under the table and drop the tablecloth over the remaining end of the sofa.* MISS FURNIVAL *sits serenely unknowing between the two covers.*)

Hey, what was that?

BRINDSLEY. (*Babbling.*) A draught. No match stays alight in this room. It's impossible. Cross currents, you know. Old houses are full of them. They're almost a permanent feature in this house . . .

HAROLD. (*Bewildered.*) I don't know what you're on about. (HE *strikes another match.*)

(BRINDSLEY *again blows it out as* HE *nips over to sit in the chair downstage left, but this time is seen.*)

HAROLD. What's up with you?

BRINDSLEY. Nothing!

HAROLD. Have you got a dead body in here or something?

BRINDSLEY. NO! (HE *starts his maniacal laughter.*)

HAROLD. Here, have you been drinking?

BRINDSLEY. No. Of course not.

(HAROLD *strikes another match.* BRINDSLEY *dashes up. All these strikings and blowings are of course accompanied by swift and violent alterations of the light.*)

HAROLD. (*Exasperated.*) Now look here! What's up with you?

BRINDSLEY. (*Inspired.*) Dangerous!

HAROLD. What?

BRINDSLEY. (*Frantically improvising.*) Dangerous! It's danger-

[69]

ous! . . . We can all die! Naked flames! Hideous accidents can happen with naked flames!

HAROLD. I don't know what you're on about—what's up with you?

(BRINDSLEY *clutches* HAROLD *and backs him bewilderedly across to the center table.*)

BRINDSLEY. I've just remembered! It's something they always warn you about. In old houses the fuse box and the gas meter are in the same cupboard. They are here!

COLONEL. So what about it?

BRINDSLEY. Well . . . electrical blowouts can damage the gas supply. They're famous for it. They do it all the time! And they say you've got to avoid naked flames till they're mended.

COLONEL. I've never heard of that.

HAROLD. Me neither.

BRINDSLEY. Well, take my word for it. It's fantastically danger-ous to burn a naked flame in this room!

CAROL. (*Catching on.*) Brin's absolutely right. In fact, they warned me about it on the phone this evening when I called them. They said, "Whatever you do, don't strike a match till the fuse is mended."

BRINDSLEY. There, you see!—it's terribly dangerous.

COLONEL. (*Grimly.*) Then why didn't you warn me, Dumpling?

CAROL. I—I forgot.

COLONEL. Brilliant!

MISS FURNIVAL. Oh goodness, we must take care.

BRINDSLEY. We certainly must! . . . (*Pause.*) Let's all have a drink. Cheer us up! . . .

CAROL. Good idea! Mr. Gorringe, would you like a drink?

HAROLD. Well, I must say, that wouldn't come amiss. Not after the journey I've had tonight. I swear to God there was thirty-five people in that compartment if there was one—babes in arms, toddlers, two nuns, three yapping poodles, and not a sausage to eat from Leamington to London. It's a bloody disgrace.

MISS FURNIVAL. You'd think they'd put on a restaurant car, Mr. Gorringe.

HAROLD. Not them, Ferny. They don't care if you perish once they've got your fare. Excuse me, I'll just go and clean up.

BRINDSLEY. (*Panic.*) You can do that here.

HAROLD. Well, I must unpack anyway.

BRINDSLEY. Do it later.

HAROLD. No, I hate to keep clothes in a suitcase longer than I absolutely have to. If there's one thing I can't stand, it's a creased suit.

BRINDSLEY. Five more minutes won't hurt, surely?

HAROLD. Ooh, you aren't half bossy!

CAROL. What will you have? Winnie, Vera or Ginette?

HAROLD. Come again?

CAROL. Winnie Whiskey, Vera Vodka, or dear old standby Ginette.

HAROLD. (*Yielding.*) I can see you're the camp one! . . . If it's all the same to you, I'll have a drop of Ginette, please, and a little lime juice.

COLONEL. Young man, do I have to keep reminding you that you are in an emergency? You have a guest arrivin' any second.

BRINDSLEY. Oh God, I'd forgotten!

COLONEL. Try the pub. Try the neighbors. Try who you damn well please, sir—but *get a torch!*

BRINDSLEY. Yes . . . Yes! . . . Carol, can I have a word with you, please?

CAROL. I'm here.

(SHE *gropes toward him and* BRINDSLEY *leads her to the stairs.*)

COLONEL. What now?

BRINDSLEY. Excuse us just a moment, please, Colonel.

(HE *pulls her quickly after him, up the stairs.*)

MISS FURNIVAL. (*As* THEY *do this.*) Oh, Mr. Gorringe, it's so exciting. You'll never guess who's coming here tonight.

HAROLD. Who?

MISS FURNIVAL. Guess.

HAROLD. The Queen!

MISS FURNIVAL. Oh, Mr. Gorringe, you are ridiculous!

(BRINDSLEY *arrives at the top of the stairs, then opens the bedroom door and closes it behind them.*)

BRINDSLEY. What are we going to do?

CAROL. (*Behind the door.*) I don't know!

BRINDSLEY. (*Behind the door.*) Think!

CAROL. But—

BRINDSLEY. *Think!*

COLONEL. Is that boy touched or somethin'?

HAROLD. Touched? He's an absolute poppet.

COLONEL. A what?

HAROLD. A duck. I've known him for years, ever since he came here. There's not many secrets we keep from each other, I can tell you.

COLONEL. (*Frostily.*) Really?

HAROLD. Yes, really. He's a very sweet boy.

(BRINDSLEY *and* CAROL *emerge from behind the bedroom door.*)

BRINDSLEY. We'll have to put all Harold's furniture back in his room.

CAROL. *Now?!*

BRINDSLEY. We'll have to. I can't get a torch till we do.

CAROL. We can't!

BRINDSLEY. We must. He'll go mad if he finds out what we've done.

HAROLD. Well come on, Ferny: don't be a tease. Who is it? Who's coming?

MISS FURNIVAL. I'll give you a clue. It's someone with money.

HAROLD. Money? . . . Let me think.

COLONEL. (*Calling out.*) Carol!

CAROL. Look, can't you just tell him it was a joke?

BRINDSLEY. You don't know him. He can't bear anyone to touch his treasures. They're like children to him. He cleans everything twice a day with a special swansdown duster. He'd wreck everything. Would you like him to call me a thief in front of your father?

CAROL. Of course not!

BRINDSLEY. Well, he would. He gets absolutely hysterical. I've seen him.

COLONEL. (*Mildly.*) Brindsley!

CAROL. Well, how the hell can we do it?

HAROLD. It's no good. You can't hear up there.

BRINDSLEY. (*Stripping off his jacket.*) Look, you hold the fort. Serve them drinks. Just keep things going. Leave it all to me. I'll try and put everything back in the dark.

CAROL. It won't work.

BRINDSLEY. It's *got* to!

COLONEL. (*Roaring.*) Brindsley!!

BRINDSLEY. (*Dashing to the door.*) Coming, sir . . . (*With false calm.*) I'm just getting some empties to take to the pub.

COLONEL. Say what you like. That boy's touched.

BRINDSLEY. (*To* CAROL, *intimately.*) Trust me, darling.

(THEY *kiss.*)

[73]

COLONEL. At the double, Miller.

BRINDSLEY. Yes, sir! Yes, sir!

(HE *rushes out and in his anxiety*, HE *misses his footing and falls neatly down the entire flight of stairs.*
Picking himself up.)

I'm off now, Colonel! Help is definitely on the way.

COLONEL. Well, hurry it up, man.

BRINDSLEY. Carol will give you drinks. If Mr. Bamberger arrives, just explain the situation to him.

HAROLD. (*Feeling for his hand.*) Would you like me to come with you?

BRINDSLEY. No, no, no—good heavens: stay and enjoy yourself.

(HAROLD *kisses his hand.* BRINDSLEY *pulls it away.*)

I mean, you must be exhausted after all those poodles. A nice gin and lime will do wonders. I shan't be a minute.

(HE *reaches the door, opens it, then slams it loudly, remaining on the inside. Stealthily* HE *opens it again, stands dead still for a moment, center, silently indicating to himself the position of the chairs* HE *has to move—then* HE *finds his way to the first of the Regency chairs, downstage left, which* HE *lifts noiselessly.*)

CAROL. (*With bright desperation.*) Well now, drinks! What's everyone going to have? It's Ginette for Mr. Gorringe and I suppose Winnie for Daddy.

COLONEL. And how on earth are you going to do that in the dark?

CAROL. I remember the exact way I put out the bottles.

(BRINDSLEY *bumps into her with the chair and falls back, gored by its leg.*)

CAROL. It's very simple.

HAROLD. Oh look, luv, let me strike a match. I'm sure it's not that dangerous, just for a minute. (HE *strikes a match.*)

CAROL. Oh no! . . .

(BRINDSLEY *ducks down, chair in hand, and blows out the match.*)

Do you want to blow us all up, Mr. Gorringe? . . . All poor Mr. Bamberger would find would be teensy weensy bits of us. Very messypegs.

(SHE *snatches the box of matches, feels for the ice bucket, and drops them into it.* BRINDSLEY *steals out, Felix-the-cat-like, with the chair as* CAROL *fumblingly starts to mix drinks.* HE *sets it down, opens* HAROLD'S *door, and disappears inside it with the chair.*)

HAROLD. Bamberger? Is that who's coming? Georg Bamberger?

MISS FURNIVAL. Yes. To see Mr. Miller's work. Isn't it exciting?

HAROLD. Well, I never. I read an article about him last week in the Sunday Pic. He's known as the mystery millionaire. He's almost completely deaf—deaf as a post, and spends most of his time indoors alone with his collection. He hardly ever goes out, except to a gallery or a private studio. That's the life! If I had money that's what I'd do. Just collect all the china and porcelain I wanted.

(BRINDSLEY *returns with a poor, broken-down chair of his own and sets it down in the same position as the one* HE *has taken out. The second chair presents a harder challenge. It sits right across the room, upstage right. Delicately* HE *moves towards it—but* HE *has difficulty finding it. We watch him walk round and round it in desperately narrowing circles till* HE *touches it and with relief picks it up.*)

MISS FURNIVAL. I've never met a millionaire. I've always wondered if they feel different to us. I mean their actual skins.

COLONEL. Their skins?

MISS FURNIVAL. Yes. I've always imagined they must be softer than ours. Like the skins of ladies when I was a girl.

CAROL. What an interesting idea.

HAROLD. Oh she's very fanciful is Ferny. Real imagination, I always say.

MISS FURNIVAL. Very kind of you, Mr. Gorringe. You're always so generous with your compliments.

(As SHE *speaks her next speech staring smugly into the darkness, hands clasped in maidenly gentility, the second Regency chair is being moved slowly across what should be her field of vision, two inches from her face. During the following,* BRINDSLEY *unfortunately misaims and carries the chair past the door, bumps into the wall, retreats from it, and inadvertently shuts the door softly with his back. Now* HE *cannot get out of the room.* HE *has to set down the chair, grope for the door handle, turn it, then open the door—then re-find the chair which* HE *has quite lost. This takes a long and frantic time. At last* HE *triumphs, and staggers from the room, nearly exhausted.*)

But this is by no means fancy. In my day, softness of skin was quite the sign of refinement. Nowadays, of course, it's hard enough for us middle classes to keep ourselves decently clothed, let alone soft. My father used to say, even before the bombs came and burnt our dear little house at Wendover: "The game's up, my girl. We middle classes are as dead as the dodo." Poor Father, how right he was.

———

NOTE: *Hopefully, if the counterpoint of farce action goes well,* MISS FURNIVAL *may have to ad-lib a fair bit during all this, and not mind too much if nobody hears her. The essential thing for all four actors during the furniture-moving is to preserve the look of ordinary conversation.*

COLONEL. Your father was a professional man?

MISS FURNIVAL. He was a man of God, Colonel.

COLONEL. Oh.

(BRINDSLEY *returns with a broken-down rocking chair of his own.* HE *crosses gingerly to where the* COLONEL *is sitting.*)

How are those drinks coming, Dumpling?

CAROL. Fine, Daddy. They'll be one minute.

COLONEL. (*Speaking directly into* BRINDSLEY'S *face.*) Let me help you.

(BRINDSLEY *staggers back, startled.*)

CAROL. You can take this bitter lemon to Miss Furnival if you want.

(BRINDSLEY *sets down the rocker immediately next to the* COLONEL'S *chair.*)

COLONEL. Very well.

(HE *rises just as* BRINDSLEY'S *hand pulls it from beneath him. With his other hand* BRINDSLEY *pulls the rocker into the identical position. The* COLONEL *moves slowly across the room, arms outstretched for the bitter lemon. Unknowingly* BRINDSLEY *follows him, carrying the third chair. The* COLONEL *collides gently with the table. At the same moment* BRINDS- LEY *reaches it upstage of him, and searches for the Wedg- wood bowl. Their hands narrowly miss. Then the* YOUNG MAN *remembers the bowl is under the table. Deftly* HE *reaches down and retrieves it—and carrying it in one hand and the chair in the other, triumphantly leaves the room through the arch unconsciously provided by the outstretched arms of* CAROL *and the* COLONEL, *giving and receiving a glass of Scotch—which* THEY *think is lemonade.*)

CAROL. Here you are, Daddy. Bitter lemon for Miss Furnival.

COLONEL. Right you are, Dumpling. (*To* MISS FURNIVAL.) So your father was a minister then?

MISS FURNIVAL. He was a saint, Colonel. I'm only thankful he never lived to see the rudeness and vulgarity of life today.

(*The* COLONEL *sets off to find her but goes much too far to the right.*)

HAROLD. (HE *sits on the sofa beside her.*) Oooh, you're so right, Ferny. Rudeness and vulgarity—that's it to a T. The manners of some people today are beyond belief. Honestly. Did I tell you what happened in my shop last Friday? I don't think I did.

MISS FURNIVAL. No, Mr. Gorringe, I don't think so.

(*Her voice corrects the* COLONEL'S *direction. During the following* HE *moves slowly up toward her.*)

HAROLD. Well, I'd just opened up—it was about quarter to ten and I was dusting off the teapots—you know, Rockingham collects the dust something shocking!—when who should walk in but that Mrs. Levitt, you know—the ginger-haired bit I told you about, the one who thinks she's God's gift to bachelors.

COLONEL. (*Finding her head with his hand and presenting her with the Scotch.*) Here's your lemonade.

MISS FURNIVAL. Oh, thank you. Most kind.

(*Throughout* HAROLD'S *story,* MISS FURNIVAL *nurses the glass, not drinking. The* COLONEL *finds his way slowly back to the chair* HE *thinks* HE *was sitting on before, but which is now a rocker.* BRINDSLEY *re-appears triumphantly carrying one of the original Regency chairs* HE *took out.* HE *moves slowly across the room getting his bearings.*)

HAROLD. Anyway, she's got in her hand a vase I'd sold her last week—it was a birthday present for an old geezer she's having a bit of a ding dong with somewhere in Earls Court, hoping to collect all his lolly when he dies, as I read the situation. I'm a pretty good judge of character, Ferny, as you know—and she's a real grasper if ever I saw one.

(*The* COLONEL *sits heavily in the rocking chair which over-balances backward, spilling him onto the floor.*)

COLONEL. Dammit to hell!

CAROL. What's the matter, Daddy?

(*A pause.* BRINDSLEY *sits down panic-stricken on the chair* HE *has carried in. The* COLONEL *feels the chair and sets it on its feet.*)

COLONEL. (*Unbelieving.*) It's a blasted rockin' chair! I didn't see a blasted rockin' chair here before! . . .

(*Astounded, the* COLONEL *remains on the floor.* BRINDSLEY *rises and moves the chair to the original position of the second chair* HE *moved.*)

HAROLD. Oh yes, you want to watch that. It's in a pretty ropey condition, I've told Brin about it several times. Anyway, this vase. It's a nice bit of Kang Tsi, blue and white with a good orange-peel glaze, absolutely authentic—I'd let her have it for twenty-five pounds, and she'd got infinitely the best of the bargain, no argument about that.

(HAROLD *rises and leans against the center table to tell his story more effectively. The* COLONEL *seats himself again, gingerly.*)

Well, in she prances, her hair all done up in one of them bouffon hair-dos, you know, tarty—French-like—it would have looked fancy on a girl half her age with twice her looks—

(BRINDSLEY *mistakenly lifts the end of the sofa.* MISS FURNIVAL *gives a little scream at the jolt.*)

HAROLD. Exactly. You know the sort.

(BRINDSLEY *staggers in the opposite direction downstage onto the rostrum.*)

And d'you know what she says to me? "Mr. Gorringe," she says, "I've been cheated."

MISS FURNIVAL. No!

BLACK COMEDY

HAROLD. Her very words. "Cheated."

(BRINDSLEY *collides with the sculpture on the dais. It jangles violently.*

To it.)

Hush up, I'm talking!

CAROL. (*Covering up.*) I'm frightfully sorry.

(HAROLD *whirls round, surprised.*)

HAROLD. Anyway—"Oh, I say, and how exactly has that occurred, Mrs. Levitt?" "Well," she says, "quite by chance I took this vase over to Bill Everett in the Portobello, and he says it's not what you called it at all, Chinese and very rare. He says it's a piece of nineteenth-century English trash."

(BRINDSLEY *finds the lamp on the downstage table and picks it up.* HE *walks with it round the rocking chair, on which the* COLONEL *is now sitting again.*)

"Does he?" I say. "Does he?" I keep calm. I always do when I'm riled. "Yes," she says. "He does. And I'd thank you to give me money back."

(*The wire of the lamp has followed* BRINDSLEY *round the bottom of the rocking chair. It catches.* BRINDSLEY *tugs it gently. The chair moves. Surprised, the* COLONEL *jerks forward.* BRINDSLEY *tugs it again, much harder. The rocking chair is pulled forward, spilling the* COLONEL *out of it, again onto the floor, and then falling itself on top of him. The shade of the lamp comes off. During the ensuing dialogue* BRINDSLEY *gets to his knees and crawls right across the room following the flex of the lamp.* HE *finds the plug, pulls it out, and—still on his knees—re-traces his steps, winding up the wire around his arm, and becoming helplessly entangled in it. The* COLONEL *remains on the floor, now really alarmed.*)

MISS FURNIVAL. How dreadful, Mr. Gorringe. What did you do?

HAROLD. I counted to ten, and then I let her have it. "In the

[80]

first place," I said, "I don't expect my customers to go checking up on my honesty behind my back. In the second, Bill Everett is ignorant as Barnsley dirt, he doesn't know Tang from Ting. And in the third place, that applies to you, too, Mrs. Levitt."

MISS FURNIVAL. You didn't!

HAROLD. I certainly did—and worse than that. "You've got in your hand," I said, "a minor masterpiece of Chinese pottery. But in point of fact," I said, "you're not even fit to hold a 1953 Coronation mug. Don't you ever come in here again," I said, "—don't you cross my threshold. Because if you do, Mrs. Levitt, I won't make myself responsible for the consequences."

CAROL. (*With two drinks in her hand.*) My, Mr. Gorringe, how splendid of you. Here's your gin and lime. You deserve it. (SHE *hands him the bitter lemon.*)

HAROLD. (*Accepting it.*) Ta. I was proper blazing, I didn't care.

CAROL. Where are you? Where are you, Daddy? Here's your Scotch.

COLONEL. Here, Dumpling!

(HE *gets up dazedly and fumbles his way to the glass of gin and lime.* BRINDSLEY *meanwhile realizes* HE *has lost the shade of the lamp. On his knees,* HE *begins to look for it.*)

HAROLD. Carrotty old bitch—telling *me* about pottery! *Oooh!!* (HE *shakes himself indignantly at the recollection of it.*)

MISS FURNIVAL. Do you care for porcelain yourself, Colonel?

COLONEL. I'm afraid I don't know very much about it, Madam. I like some of that Chinese stuff—you get some lovely colors, like on that statue I saw when I came in here—very delicate.

HAROLD. What statue's that, Colonel?

COLONEL. The one on the packing case, sir. Very fine.

HAROLD. I didn't know Brin had any Chinese stuff. What's it of then, this statue?

(BRINDSLEY *freezes*.)

CAROL. (*Desperately*.) Well, we've all got drinks, I'd like to propose Daddy's regimental toast. Raise your glasses everyone! "To the dear old Twenty-Fifth Horse. Up the British, and Death to All Natives"!

MISS FURNIVAL. I'll drink to that!

HAROLD. Up the old Twenty-Fifth!!

(*Quickly* BRINDSLEY *finds the Buddha, moves it from the packing case to the table, then gets* HAROLD's *raincoat from the sofa, and wraps the statue up in it, leaving it on the table*.)

COLONEL. Thank you, Dumpling. That was very touchin' of you. Very touchin' indeed. (HE *swallows his drink*.) Dammit, that's gin!

HAROLD. I've got lemonade!

MISS FURNIVAL. Oh! Horrible! . . . Quite horrible! That would be alcohol, I suppose! . . . Oh dear, how unpleasant! . . .

HAROLD. (*To* MISS FURNIVAL.) Here, luv, exchange with me. No —you get the lemonade—but I get the gin. Colonel—

COLONEL. Here, sir.

(*Seizing her chance* MISS FURNIVAL *downs a huge draft of Scotch*. THEY *all exchange drinks*. BRINDSLEY *resumes his frantic search for the shade*.)

HAROLD. Here, Ferny.

(*The* COLONEL *hands her the gin and lime*. HE *gets instead the bitter lemon from* HAROLD. HAROLD *gets the Scotch*.)

MISS FURNIVAL. Thank you.

HAROLD. Well, let's try again. Bottoms up!

COLONEL. Quite.

(THEY *drink. Triumphantly,* BRINDSLEY *finds the shade. Un-*

fortunately at the same moment the COLONEL *spits out his lemonade in a fury all over him, as he marches toward him on his knees.*)

Look here—I can't stand another minute of this!

(HE *fishes his lighter out of his pocket and angrily tries to light it.*)

CAROL. Daddy, please!

COLONEL. I don't care, Dumpling. If I blow us up, then I'll blow us up! This is ridiculous . . .

(*His words die in the flame.* HE *spies* BRINDSLEY *kneeling at his feet, wound about with lampwire.*)

What the devil are you doin' there?

BRINDSLEY. (*Blowing out his lighter.*) Now don't be rash, Colonel! Isn't the first rule of an officer "Don't involve your men in unnecessary danger"?

(*Quickly* HE *steals, still on his knees, to the table downstage right.*)

COLONEL. Don't be impertinent. Where's the torch?

BRINDSLEY. Er . . . the pub was closed.

HAROLD. You didn't go to the pub in that time, surely? You couldn't have done.

BRINDSLEY. Of course I did.

MISS FURNIVAL. But it's five streets away, Mr. Miller.

BRINDSLEY. Needs must when the devil drives, Miss Furnival. Whatever that means.

(*Quickly* HE *lifts the table, and steals out of the room with it and the wrecked lamp.*)

COLONEL. (*Who thinks* HE *is still kneeling at his feet.*) Now look here: there's somethin' very peculiar goin' on in this room. I may not know about art, Miller, but I know men. I know a liar in the light, and I know one in the dark.

CAROL. Daddy!

COLONEL. I don't want to doubt your word, sir. All the same, I'd like your oath you went out to that public house. *Well?*

CAROL. (*Realizing* HE *isn't there, raising her voice.*) Brin, Daddy's talking to you!

COLONEL. What are you shoutin' for?

BRINDSLEY. (*Rushing back from* HAROLD's *room, still entangled in the lamp.*) Of course. I know. He's absolutely right. I was—just thinking it over for a moment.

COLONEL. Well? What's your answer?

BRINDSLEY. I . . . I couldn't agree with you more, sir.

COLONEL. What?

BRINDSLEY. That was a very perceptive remark you made there. Not everyone would have thought of that. Individual. You know. Almost witty. Well, it *was* witty. Why be ungenerous? . . .

COLONEL. Look, young man, are you trying to be funny?

BRINDSLEY. (*Ingratiatingly.*) Well, I'll try anything once . . .

HAROLD. I say, this is becoming a bit unpleasant, isn't it?

CAROL. It's becoming drearypegs.

COLONEL. Quiet, Dumpling. Let me handle this.

BRINDSLEY. What's there to handle, sir?

COLONEL. If you think I'm going to let my daughter marry a born liar, you're very much mistaken.

HAROLD. Marry!

CAROL. Well, that's the idea.

HAROLD. You and this young lady, Brin?

CAROL. Are what's laughingly known as engaged. Subject of course to Daddy's approval.

HAROLD. Well! (*Furious at the news, and at the fact that* BRINDSLEY *hasn't confided in him.*) What a surprise! . . .

BRINDSLEY. We were keeping it a secret.

HAROLD. Evidently. How long's this been going on, then?

BRINDSLEY. A few months.

HAROLD. You old slyboots.

BRINDSLEY. (*Nervous.*) I hope you approve, Harold.

HAROLD. Well, I must say, you know how to keep things to yourself.

BRINDSLEY. (*Placatingly.*) I meant to tell you, Harold . . . I really did. You were the one person I was going to tell.

HAROLD. Well why didn't you, then?

BRINDSLEY. I don't know. I just never got around to it.

HAROLD. You saw me every day.

BRINDSLEY. I know.

HAROLD. You could have mentioned it at any time.

BRINDSLEY. I know.

HAROLD. (*Huffy.*) Well, it's your business. There's no obligation to share confidences. I've only been your neighbor for three years. I've always assumed there was more than a geographical closeness between us, but I was obviously mistaken.

BRINDSLEY. Oh don't start getting huffy, Harold.

HAROLD. I'm not getting anything. I'm just saying it's surprising, that's all. Surprising and somewhat disappointing.

BRINDSLEY. Oh look, Harold, please understand—

HAROLD. (*Shrill.*) There's no need to say anything! It'll just teach me in future not to bank too much on friendship. It's silly me again! Silly, stupid, trusting me!

(MISS FURNIVAL *rises in agitation and gropes her way to the drinks table.*)

COLONEL. Good God!

CAROL. (*Wheedling.*) Oh come, Mr. Gorringe. We haven't told anybody. Not one single soulipegs. Really.

COLONEL. At the moment, Dumpling, there's nothing to tell. And I'm not sure there's going to be!

BRINDSLEY. Look, sir, we seem to have got off on the wrong foot. If it's my fault, I apologize.

MISS FURNIVAL. (*Groping about on the drinks table.*) My father always used to say, "To err is human: to forgive divine."

CAROL. I thought that was somebody else.

MISS FURNIVAL. (*Blithely.*) So many people copied him. (SHE *finds the open bottle of gin, lifts it and sniffs it eagerly.*)

CAROL. May I help you, Miss Furnival?

MISS FURNIVAL. No, thank you, Miss Melkett. I'm just getting myself another bitter lemon. That is—if I may, Mr. Miller?

BRINDSLEY. Of course. Help yourself.

MISS FURNIVAL. Thank you, most kind!

(SHE *pours more gin into her glass and returns slowly to sit upstage on the edge of the rostrum.*)

COLONEL. Well, sir, wherever you are—

BRINDSLEY. Here, Colonel.

COLONEL. I'll overlook your damn peculiar behavior this once, but understand this, Miller. My daughter's dear to me. You show me you can look after her, and I'll consider the whole thing most favorably. I can't say fairer than that, can I?

BRINDSLEY. No, sir. Most fair, sir. Most fair. (HE *pulls a hideous face one inch from the* COLONEL'S.)

CAROL. Of course he can look after me, Daddy. His works are going to be world-famous. In five years I'll feel just like Mrs. Michaelangelo.

HAROLD. (*Loftily.*) There wasn't a Mrs. Michaelangelo, actually.

CAROL. (*Irritated.*) Wasn't there?

HAROLD. No. He had passionate feelings of a rather different nature.

CAROL. Really, Mr. Gorringe. I didn't know that. (SHE *puts out her tongue at him.*)

BRINDSLEY. Look, Harold, I'm sorry if I've hurt your feelings.

HAROLD. (*Loftily.*) You haven't.

BRINDSLEY. I know I have. Please forgive me.

CAROL. Oh, do, Mr. Gorringe. Quarreling is so dreary. I hope we're all going to be great friends.

HAROLD. I'm not sure that I can contemplate a friendly relationship with a viper.

MISS FURNIVAL. Remember: to err is human, to forgive divine!

COLONEL. (*Irritated.*) You just said that, madam.

(CLEA *enters, wearing dark glasses and carrying an air-bag.* SHE *stands in the doorway, amazed by the dark.* SHE *takes off her glasses, but this doesn't improve matters.*)

MISS FURNIVAL. (*Downing her gin happily.*) Did I?

CAROL. Brin's not really a viper. He's just artistic, aren't you, darling?

BRINDSLEY. Yes, darling.

(CAROL *sends him an audible kiss across the astonished* CLEA. HE *returns it, equally audibly.*)

CAROL. (*Winningly.*) Come on, Mr. Gorringe. It really is a case of forgive and forgettipegs.

HAROLD. Is it reallypegs?

CAROL. Have another Ginette and lime. I'll have one with you. (SHE *rises and mixes the drink.*)

HAROLD. (*Rising.*) Oh, all right. I don't mind if I do.

CAROL. Let me mix it for you.

HAROLD. Ta.

(HE *crosses to her, narrowly missing* CLEA *who is now crossing the room to the sofa, and gets his drink.*)

I must say there's nothing nicer than having a booze up with a pretty girl.

CAROL. (*Archly.*) You haven't seen me yet.

HAROLD. Oh, I just know it. Brindsley always had wonderful

taste. I've often said to him, you've got the same taste in ladies as I have in porcelain. Ta.

(HAROLD *and* BRINDSLEY—*one from upstage, one from across the room—begin to converge on the sofa. On the word "modest"* ALL THREE, CLEA *in the middle, sit on it.* BRINDSLEY *of course imagines* HE *is sitting next to* HAROLD.)

BRINDSLEY. Harold!

CAROL. Oh don't be silly, Brin. Why be so modest? I found a photograph of one of his bits from two years ago, and I must say she was pretty stunning in a blowsy sort of way.

HAROLD. Which one was that, then? I suppose she means Clea.

CAROL. Did you know her, Mr. Gorringe?

HAROLD. Oh yes. She's been around a long time.

(BRINDSLEY *nudges* CLEA *warningly—imagining* SHE *is* HAROLD. CLEA *gently bumps* HAROLD.)

CAROL. (*Surprised.*) Has she?

HAROLD. Oh yes, dear. Or am I speaking out of turn?

BRINDSLEY. Not at all. I've told Carol all about Clea. (HE *bangs* CLEA *again, a little harder—who correspondingly bumps against* HAROLD.) Though I must say, Harold, I'm surprised you call three months "a long time."

(CLEA *shoots him a look of total outrage at this lie.* HAROLD *is also astonished.*)

CAROL. What was she like?

BRINDSLEY. (*Meaningfully, into* CLEA's *ear.*) I suppose you can hardly remember her, Harold.

HAROLD. (*Speaking across her.*) Why on earth shouldn't I?

BRINDSLEY. Well, since it was two years ago, you've probably forgotten.

HAROLD. Two years?!

BRINDSLEY. *Two years ago!*

(HE *punches* CLEA *so hard that the rebound knocks* HAROLD *off the sofa, drink and all.*)

HAROLD. (*Picking himself up. Spitefully.*) Well, now since you mention it, I remember her perfectly. I mean, she's not one you can easily forget!

CAROL. Was she pretty?

HAROLD. No, not at all. In fact, I'd say the opposite. Actually she was rather plain.

BRINDSLEY. She wasn't!

HAROLD. I'm just giving my opinion.

BRINDSLEY. You've never given it before.

HAROLD. (*Leaning over* CLEA.) I was never asked! But since it's come up, I always thought she was ugly. For one thing, she had teeth like a picket fence—yellow and spiky. And for another, she had bad skin.

BRINDSLEY. She had nothing of the kind!

HAROLD. She did. I remember it perfectly. It was like new pink wallpaper, with an old gray crumbly paper underneath.

MISS FURNIVAL. Quite right, Mr. Gorringe. I hardly ever saw her, but I do recall her skin. It was a strange color, as you say —and very coarse . . . Not soft, as the skins of young ladies should be, if they *are* young ladies.

(CLEA *rises in outrage.*)

HAROLD. Aye, that's right. Coarse.

MISS FURNIVAL. And rather lumpy.

HAROLD. Very lumpy.

BRINDSLEY. This is disgraceful.

HAROLD. You knew I never liked her, Brindsley. She was too clever by half.

MISS FURNIVAL. And so tiresomely Bohemian.

CAROL. You mean she was as pretentious as her name?

(CLEA, *who has been reacting to this last exchange of comments about her like a spectator at a tennis match, now reacts to* CAROL *open-mouthed.*)

I bet she was. That photograph I found showed her in a

dirndl and a sort of sultry peasant blouse. She looked like
"The Bartered Bride" done by Lloyds Bank.

(THEY *laugh,* BRINDSLEY *hardest of all. Guided by the noise,*
CLEA *aims her hand and slaps his face.*)

BRINDSLEY. Ahh!

CAROL. What's wrong?

MISS FURNIVAL. What is it, Mr. Miller?

BRINDSLEY. (*Furious.*) That's not very funny, Harold. What
the hell's the matter with you?

(CLEA *makes her escape.*)

HAROLD. (*Indignant.*) With me?

BRINDSLEY. Well, I'm sure it wasn't the Colonel.

COLONEL. What wasn't, sir?

(BRINDSLEY, *groping about, catches* CLEA *by the bottom, and
instantly recognizes it.*)

BRINDSLEY. *Clea!* . . . (*In horror.*) *Clea!!*

(CLEA *breaks loose and moves away from him. During the
following* HE *tries to find her in the dark, and* SHE *narrowly
avoids him.*)

COLONEL. What?

BRINDSLEY. I was just remembering her, sir. You're all talking
the most awful nonsense. She was beautiful . . . And anyway, Harold, you just said I was famous for my taste in
women.

HAROLD. Aye, but it had its lapses.

BRINDSLEY. (*Frantically moving about.*) Rubbish! She was
beautiful and tender and considerate and kind and loyal and
witty and adorable in every way!

CAROL. You told me she was as cozy as a steel razor blade.

BRINDSLEY. Did I? Surely not! No. What I said was . . . something quite different . . . Utterly different . . . entirely different . . . As different as chalk from cheese. Although when

you come to think of it, cheese isn't all that different from chalk. (HE *gives his braying laugh.*)

COLONEL. Are you sure you know what you're talking about?

(*During this* CLEA *has reached the table, picked up a bottle of Scotch, and rejected it in favor of vodka, which* SHE *takes with her.*)

CAROL. You said to me in this room when I asked you what she was like, "She was a painter. Very honest. Very clever, and just about as cozy—"

BRINDSLEY. (*Stopping, exasperated.*) As a steel razor blade! Well then, I said it! So bloody what? . . .

CAROL. So nothing!

(HE *throws out his hands in a gesture of desperate exhaustion and bumps straight into* CLEA. THEY *instantly embrace,* CLEA *twining herself around him, her vodka bottle held aloft. A tiny pause.*)

COLONEL. If that boy isn't touched, I don't know the meaning of the word!

CAROL. What's all this talk about her being kind and tender, all of a sudden?

BRINDSLEY. (*Tenderly, holding* CLEA.) She could be. On occasion. Very.

CAROL. Very rare occasions, I imagine.

BRINDSLEY. Not so rare. (HE *kisses* CLEA *again.*) Not so rare at all. (HE *leads her softly past the irritated* CAROL, *toward the stairs.*)

CAROL. Meaning what, exactly? . . . (*Shouting.*) Brindsley, I'm talking to you!

BRINDSLEY. (*Sotto voce, into* CLEA'S *ear as* THEY *stand just behind* HAROLD.) I can explain. Go up to the bedroom. Wait for me there.

[91]

HAROLD. (*In amazement: thinking* HE *is being addressed.*) Now? Do you think this is quite the moment?

BRINDSLEY. Oh God! . . . I wasn't talking to you.

CAROL. What did you say?

HAROLD. (*To* CAROL.) I think he wants *you* upstairs. (*Slyly.*) For what purpose, I can't begin to imagine.

COLONEL. They're going to do some more of that plotting, I daresay.

MISS FURNIVAL. Lover's talk, Colonel.

COLONEL. Very touching, I'm sure.

(BRINDSLEY *pushes* CLEA *ahead of him up the stairs.*)

MISS FURNIVAL. "Journeys end in lovers meeting," as my father always used to say.

COLONEL. What a strikingly original father you seem to have had, madam.

(CAROL *joins the* OTHER TWO *on the stairs. We see* ALL THREE *groping blindly up to the bedroom,* BRINDSLEY'S *hands on* CLEA'S *hips,* CAROL'S *on* BRINDSLEY'S.)

CAROL. (*With a conspirator's stage whisper.*) What is it, darling? Has something gone wrong? What can't you move?

(*This next dialogue sotto voce.*)

BRINDSLEY. Nothing. It's all back—every bit of it—except the sofa, and I've covered that up.

CAROL. You mean, we can have lights?

BRINDSLEY. Yes . . . NO!!

CAROL. Why not?

BRINDSLEY. Never mind!

CAROL. Why do you want me in the bedroom?

BRINDSLEY. I don't. Go away!

CAROL. Charming!

BRINDSLEY. I didn't mean that.

COLONEL. There you are. They *are* plotting again. What the hell is going on up there?

BRINDSLEY. Nothing, Colonel. I've just remembered—there may be a torch under my bed. I keep it to blind the burglars with. Have another drink, Colonel!

(HE *pushes* CLEA *into the bedroom and shuts the door.*)

COLONEL. What d'you mean another? I haven't had one yet.

MISS FURNIVAL. Oh! Poor Colonel! Let me get you one.

COLONEL. (*Rising.*) I can get one for myself, thank you. Let me get you another lemonade.

MISS FURNIVAL. (*Rising.*) No thank you, Colonel, I'll manage myself. It's good practice!

(THEY *grope toward the drinks table. Above,* CLEA *and* BRINDSLEY *sit on the bed.*)

CLEA. So this is what they mean by a blind date. What the hell is going on?

BRINDSLEY. (*Sarcastic.*) Nothing! Georg Bamberger is only coming to see my work tonight, and we've got a main fuse.

CLEA. Is that the reason for all this furtive clutching?

BRINDSLEY. Look, I can't explain things at the moment.

CLEA. Who's that—(*Debutante accent*) "frightful gel"?

BRINDSLEY. Just a friend.

CLEA. She sounded more than that.

BRINDSLEY. Well, if you must know, it's Carol. I've told you about her.

CLEA. The Idiot Deb?

BRINDSLEY. She's a very sweet girl. As a matter of fact we've become very good friends in the last six weeks.

CLEA. How good?

BRINDSLEY. Just good.

CLEA. And have you become friends with her father too?

BRINDSLEY. If it's any of your business, they just dropped in to meet Mr. Bamberger.

CLEA. What was it you wanted to tell me on the phone to-night?

BRINDSLEY. Nothing.

CLEA. You're lying!

BRINDSLEY. Ah, here comes the inquisition! Look, Clea, if you ever loved me, just slip away quietly with no more questions, and I'll come round later and explain everything, I promise.

CLEA. I don't believe you.

BRINDSLEY. Please darling . . . Please . . . Please . . . Please!! (THEY *kiss, passionately, stretched out on the bed.*)

COLONEL. (*Pouring.*) At last . . . a decent glass of Scotch. Are you getting your lemonade?

MISS FURNIVAL. (*Cheerfully pouring herself an enormous gin.*) Oh yes, thank you, Colonel!

COLONEL. I'm just wonderin' if this Bamberger fellow is goin' to show up at all. He's half an hour late already.

HAROLD. Oh! That's nothing, Colonel. Millionaires are always late. It's their thing.

MISS FURNIVAL. I'm sure you're right, Mr. Gorringe. That's how *I* imagine them. Hands like silk, and always two hours late.

CAROL. Brin's been up there a long time. What can he be doing?

HAROLD. Maybe he's got that Clea hidden away in his bed-room, and they're having a tête-à-tête!!

CAROL. What a flagrant suggestion, Mr. Gorringe.

BRINDSLEY. (*Disengaging himself.*) No one in the world kisses like you.

CLEA. I missed you so badly, Brin. I had to see you. I've thought about nothing else these past six weeks. Brin, I made the most awful mistake walking out.

[94]

BRINDSLEY. Clea—*please!*

CLEA. I mean we've known each other for four years. We can't just throw each other away like old newspapers.

BRINDSLEY. I don't see why not. You know my politics, you've heard my gossip, and you've certainly been through all my entertainment section.

CLEA. Well, how about a second edition?

BRINDSLEY. Darling, we simply can't talk about this now. Can't you trust me just for an hour?

CLEA. Of course I can, darling. You don't want me down there?

BRINDSLEY. No.

CLEA. Then I'll get undressed and go quietly to bed. When you've got rid of them all, I'll be waiting.

BRINDSLEY. That's a terrible idea!

CLEA. (*Reaching for him.*) I think it's lovely. A little happy relaxation for us both.

BRINDSLEY. (*Falling off the bed.*) I'm perfectly relaxed!

CAROL. Brindsley!

CLEA. "Too solemn for day, too sweet for night. Come not in darkness, come not in light." That's me, isn't it?

BRINDSLEY. Of course not. I just can't explain now, that's all.

CLEA. Oh, very well, you can explain later . . . in bed!

BRINDSLEY. Not tonight, Clea.

CLEA. Either that or I come down and discover your sordid secret.

BRINDSLEY. There *is* no sordid secret!

CLEA. Then you won't mind my coming down!

CAROL, COLONEL. (*Roaring together.*) BRINDSLEY!!!

BRINDSLEY. Oh God!! . . . All right, stay. Only keep quiet . . . Blackmailing bitch! (HE *emerges at the top of the stairs.*) Yes, my sweet?

CAROL. What are you doing up there? You've been an eternity!

[95]

BRINDSLEY. I . . . I . . . I'm just looking in the bathroom, my darling. You never know what you might find in that clever little cabinet.

COLONEL. (*Moving to the stairs.*) Are you trying to madden me, sir? Are you trying to put me in a fury?

BRINDSLEY. Certainly not, sir!!

COLONEL. I warn you, Miller, it's not difficult! In the old days in the regiment I was known for my furies. I was famous for my furies . . . Do you hear?

CLEA. I may sing!

(SHE *goes off into the bathroom.*)

BRINDSLEY. I may knock your teeth in!

COLONEL. What did you say?

CAROL. Brin! How dare you talk to Daddy like that!

BRINDSLEY. Oh!! I . . . I . . . I wasn't talking to Daddy like that . . .

CAROL. Then who *were* you talking to?

BRINDSLEY. I was talking to no one! Myself I was talking to! I was saying . . . "If I keep groping about up here like this, I might knock my teeth in!"

COLONEL. Mad! . . . Mad! . . . Mad as the south wind! It's the only explanation—you've got yourself engaged to a lunatic.

CAROL. There's something going on up there, and I'm coming up to find out what it is. Do you hear me, Brin?

BRINDSLEY. Carol—no!

CAROL. (*Climbing the stairs.*) I'm not such a fool as you take me for. I know when you're hiding something. Your voice goes all deceitful—very, very foxipegs!

BRINDSLEY. Darling please. That's not very ladylike . . . I'm sure the Colonel won't approve of you entering a man's bedroom in the dark!

(*Enter* SCHUPPANZIGH. HE *wears the overcoat and peaked cap*

[96]

*of the London Electricity Board and carries a large tool bag,
similarly labeled.*)

CAROL. I'm comin' up, Brindsley, I'm comin' up!!!

BRINDSLEY. (*Scrambling down.*) I'm coming down . . . We'll
all have a nice cozy drink . . .

SCHUPPANZIGH. 'Allo please? Mr. Miller? Mr. Miller? I've come
as was arranged.

BRINDSLEY. My God . . . it's Bamberger!

CAROL. Bamberger?

BRINDSLEY. Yes, Bamberger. (BRINDSLEY *rushes down the remaining stairs, pulling* CAROL *with him.*)

SCHUPPANZIGH. You must have thought I was never coming!
(HE *takes off his overcoat and cap.*)

BRINDSLEY. Not at all. I'm delighted you could spare the time.
I know how busy you are. I'm afraid we've had the most
idiotic disaster. We've had a fuse.

HAROLD. You'll have to speak up, dear. He's stone deaf!

BRINDSLEY. (*Yelling.*) We've had a fuse—not the best condi-
tions for seeing sculpture.

SCHUPPANZIGH. Please not to worry. Here!

(HE *produces a torch from his pocket and "lights" it. The
light on stage dims a little, as usual, to indicate this.*
ALL *relax with audible sighs of pleasure.*

SCHUPPANZIGH *at once places his tool bag on the Regency
chair, and puts his coat and cap on top of it, concealing that
it is one of* HAROLD's *chairs.*)

CAROL. Oh what a relief!

BRINDSLEY. (*Hastily dragging the sheet over the rest of the
sofa.*) Do you always travel with a torch?

SCHUPPANZIGH. Mostly, yes. It helps to see details. (*Seeing the
OTHERS.*) You are holding a private view?

MISS FURNIVAL. Oh no! I was just going. I'd hate to distract you.

SCHUPPANZIGH. Please not on my account, dear lady. I am not so easily distracted.

MISS FURNIVAL. (*Charmed.*) Oh! . . .

BRINDSLEY. (*Yelling in his ear.*) May I present Colonel Melkett?

COLONEL. (*Yelling in his other ear.*) A great honor, sir!

SCHUPPANZIGH. (*Banging his ear, to clear it.*) No, no, mine—mine!

BRINDSLEY. Miss Carol Melkett.

CAROL. (*Screeching in his ear.*) I say: hello. So glad you got here! It's terribly kind of you to take such an interest!

SCHUPPANZIGH. Not at all. *Vous êtes très gentil.*

CAROL. (*Yelling.*) What would you like to drink?

SCHUPPANZIGH. (*Bewildered.*) A little vodka, would be beautiful!

CAROL. Of course!

BRINDSLEY. Harold Gorringe—a neighbor of mine!

HAROLD. How do? Very honored, I'm sure.

SCHUPPANZIGH. Enchanted.

HAROLD. I must say it's a real thrill, meeting you!

BRINDSLEY. And another neighbor, Miss Furnival.

SCHUPPANZIGH. Enchanted.

MISS FURNIVAL. (*Hooting in his ear.*) I'm afraid we've all been taking refuge from the *storm*, as it were. (*Exclaiming as* SHE *holds* SCHUPPANZIGH's *hand.*) Oh! It *is* true! They *are* softer! Much, much softer!

SCHUPPANZIGH. (*Utterly confused as* SHE *strokes his hand.*) Softer? Please?

(BRINDSLEY *and* HAROLD *pull her away, and* SHE *subsides onto the sofa.*)

BRINDSLEY. Miss Furnival, please!

CAROL. (*At the drinks table.*) Darling, where's the vodka?

BRINDSLEY. It's on the table.

CAROL. No, it isn't.

BRINDSLEY. It must be!

(*Above,* CLEA *re-enters wearing the top half of* BRINDSLEY'S *pajamas and nothing else.* SHE *gets into bed, still clutching the vodka bottle and carrying a plastic toothmug.*)

CAROL. Well, see for yourself. There's Winnie and Ginette, and Vera has quite vanished, the naughty girl.

BRINDSLEY. She can't have done.

SCHUPPANZIGH. Please don't concern yourselves. I am pressed for time. If I might just be shown where to go.

BRINDSLEY. Of course. It's through the studio there. Darling, if you would just show our guest into the studio—*with his torch.*

CAROL. What?? . . .

BRINDSLEY. (*Sotto voce.*) *The sofa!* . . . Get him out of here.

CAROL. Oh yes!!

SCHUPPANZIGH. (*Sighting the sculpture.*) Oh! Good gracious! What an extraordinary object!

BRINDSLEY. Oh, that's just a spare piece of my work I keep in here!

SCHUPPANZIGH. Spare, maybe, but fascinating!

BRINDSLEY. You really think so?

SCHUPPANZIGH. (*Approaching it.*) I do! Ja!

BRINDSLEY. Well, in that case you should see my main collection. It's next door. My fiancée will show you!

(MISS FURNIVAL *sits on the sofa.* SHE *is now quite drunk.*)

SCHUPPANZIGH. One amazement at a time, if you please! In this gluttonous age it is easy to get visual indigestion—hard to find visual Alka Seltzer . . . Permit me to digest this first!

BRINDSLEY. Oh, by all means . . . Good, yes . . . There's no hurry—no hurry at all . . . Only . . . (*Inspired.*) Why don't you digest it *in the dark?*

SCHUPPANZIGH. I beg your pardon?

BRINDSLEY. You'll never believe it, sir, but I actually made that piece to be appreciated in the dark. I was working on a very interesting theory. You know how the Victorians said, "Children should be seen and not heard"? Well, I say, "Art should be felt and not seen."

SCHUPPANZIGH. Amazing.

BRINDSLEY. Yes, isn't it. I call it my theory of Factual Tactility. If it doesn't stab you to the quick—it's not art. Look! Why don't you give me that torch, and try for yourself?

SCHUPPANZIGH. Very well, I will!! (HE *hands* BRINDSLEY *the torch.*)

BRINDSLEY. Thank you!

(HE *turns off the torch and hands it to* CAROL. *At the same moment* MISS FURNIVAL *quietly lies down, her full length on the sofa.*)

Now just stretch out your arms and feel it all over, sir.

(HE *steals toward the studio.*)

Have a good long feel!

(SCHUPPANZIGH *embraces the metal sculpture with a fervent clash.* HE *pulls at the two metal prongs.*)

Do you see what I mean?

(*Silently* HE *opens the curtains.*)

SCHUPPANZIGH. Amazing! . . . Absolutely incredible! . . . It's quite true . . . Like this, the piece becomes a masterpiece at once.

BRINDSLEY. (*Astonished.*) It does??

SCHUPPANZIGH. But of course! I feel it here—and here—the two needles of man's unrest! . . . Self love and self hate, leading to the same point! That's the meaning of the work, isn't it?

BRINDSLEY. Of course. You've got it in one! You're obviously a great expert, sir!

(*Quietly* HE *pulls the sofa into the studio, bearing on it the supine* MISS FURNIVAL, *who waves good-bye as she disappears.*)

SCHUPPANZIGH. Not at all. V*ous êtes très gentil*—but it is evident . . . Standing here in the dark, one can feel the vital thrust of the argument! The essential anguish! The stress and the torment of our times! It is simple but not simpleminded! Ingenious, but not ingenuous! Above all, it has real moral force! Of how many modern works can one say that, good people?

CAROL. Oh, none, none at all really.

SCHUPPANZIGH. I hope I do not lecture. It can be a fault with me.

CAROL. Not at all! I could listen all night, it's so profound.

HAROLD. Me too. Really deep!

COLONEL. I don't know anything about this myself, sir, but it's an honor to listen to you.

(HE *starts off upstage in search of the sofa, seating himself tentatively in the air, then moving himself along in a sitting position, trying to find it with his rear end.*

At the same moment BRINDSLEY *emerges from the studio, closes the curtains behind him, and gropes his way to the upstage corner where there stands a small packing-case. This he carries forward, hopefully to do duty for the missing sofa. Just as* HE *places it on the ground the traveling* COLONEL *sits on it, trapping* BRINDSLEY'S *hand beneath his weight. During the following,* BRINDSLEY *tries frantically to free himself.*)

SCHUPPANZIGH. *Vous êtes très gentil!*

HAROLD. You mean to say you see all that in a bit of metal?

SCHUPPANZIGH. A *tiny* bit of metal, that's the point. A miracle of compression! You want my opinion, this boy is a genius. A master of the miniature. In the space of a matchbox he can realize anything he wants—the black virginity of Chartres! The white chorale of the Acropolis! *Wunderbar!*

CAROL. Oh how super!

SCHUPPANZIGH. You should charge immense sums for work like this, Mr. Miller. They should be very very expensive! This one, for example, how much is this?

BRINDSLEY. Fifty.

CAROL. Five hundred guineas.

SCHUPPANZIGH. Ah so! Very cheap.

HAROLD. Cheap!

CAROL. I think so, Mr. Gorringe. Well . . . so will you have it then?

SCHUPPANZIGH. Me?

BRINDSLEY. Darling . . . aren't you rushing things just a little? Perhaps you would like to see the rest of my work.

SCHUPPANZIGH. Alas, I have no more time. To linger would be pleasant, but alas, I must work . . . Also, as Moses discovered, it is sufficient to glimpse milk and honey. One does not have to wolf them down!

BRINDSLEY. Well.

COLONEL. Well . . .

HAROLD. Well. . . .

CAROL. Well . . . Would you like it then?

SCHUPPANZIGH. Very much.

COLONEL. (*Rising.* BRINDSLEY *is freed at last.*) For five hundred guineas?

SCHUPPANZIGH. Certainly—if I had it!

HAROLD. According to the Sunday Pictorial, you must be worth at least seventeen million pounds.

SCHUPPANZIGH. The Sunday papers are notoriously ill-informed. According to my bank statement, I was worth one hundred pounds, eight shillings and fourpence.

HAROLD. You mean you've gone broke?

SCHUPPANZIGH. No. I mean I never had any more.

COLONEL. Now look, sir, I know millionaires are supposed to be eccentric, but this is gettin' tiresome.

CAROL. Daddy, ssh!—

SCHUPPANZIGH. Millionaires? Who do you think I am?

COLONEL. Dammit, man!—You must know who you are!

CAROL. Mr. Bamberger, is this some kind of joke you like to play?

SCHUPPANZIGH. Excuse me. That is not my name.

BRINDSLEY. It isn't?

SCHUPPANZIGH. No. My name is Schuppanzigh. Franz Schuppanzigh. Born in Weimar 1905. Student of Philosophy at Heidelberg 1934. Refugee to this country, 1938. Regular employment ever since with the London Electricity Board.

(ALL *rise*.)

CAROL. Electricity?

MISS FURNIVAL. Electricity!

BRINDSLEY. You mean you're not?—

HAROLD. Of course he's not!

SCHUPPANZIGH. But who did you imagine I was?

HAROLD. (*Furious.*) How dare you? (HE *snatches the* ELECTRICIAN's *torch*.)

SCHUPPANZIGH. (*Retreating before him.*) Please?—

HAROLD. Of all the nerve, coming in here, giving us a lecture about needles and virgins, and all the time you're simply here to mend the fuses!

[103]

COLONEL. I agree with you, sir. It's monstrous!

SCHUPPANZIGH. (*Bewildered.*) It is?

(*The* COLONEL *takes the torch and shines it pitilessly in the* MAN's *face.*)

COLONEL. You come in here, a public servant, and proceed to harangue your employers, unasked and uninvited.

SCHUPPANZIGH. (*Bewildered.*) Excuse me. But I *was* invited.

COLONEL. Don't answer back. In my day you would have been fired on the spot for impertinence.

CAROL. Daddy's absolutely right! Ever since the Beatles, the lower classes think they can behave exactly as they want.

COLONEL. (*Handing the torch to* BRINDSLEY.) Miller, will you kindly show this feller his work?

BRINDSLEY. The mains are in the cellar. There's a trapdoor. (*Indicating.*) Do you mind?

SCHUPPANZIGH. (*Snatching the torch furiously.*) Why should I mind? It's why I came, after all! (HE *takes his coat, cap, and bag off* HAROLD's *Regency chair . . . Seeing it.*) Now there is a really beautiful chair!

(BRINDSLEY *stares at the chair aghast—and in a twinkling seats himself in it to conceal it.*)

BRINDSLEY. (*Exasperated.*) Why don't you just go into the cellar?

SCHUPPANZIGH. *How?* Where is it?

BRINDSLEY. (*To* CAROL.) Darling, will you open the trap, please.

CAROL. Me? (*Understanding—as* HE *indicates the chair.*) Oh— yes! (SHE *kneels and struggles to open the trap.*)

COLONEL. (*To* BRINDSLEY.) Well, I must say, that's very gallant of you, Miller.

BRINDSLEY. I've got a sudden touch of lumbago, sir. It often afflicts me after long spells in the dark.

CAROL. (*Very sympathetic.*) Oh, darling! Has it come back?

BRINDSLEY. I'm afraid it has, my sweet.

HAROLD. (*Opening the trap.*) Here, let me. I'm not as frail as our wilting friend. (*To* SCHUPPANZIGH.) Well, down you go, you!

SCHUPPANZIGH. (*Shrugging.*) So. Farewell. I leave the light of Art for the dark of Science.

HAROLD. Let's have a little less of your lip, shall we?

SCHUPPANZIGH. Excuse me.

(SCHUPPANZIGH *descends through the trap, taking the torch with him.* HAROLD *slams the trap door down irritably after him, and of course the lights immediately come up full. There is a long pause.* ALL *stand about embarrassed. Suddenly they hear the noise of* MISS FURNIVAL *singing "Rock of Ages" in a high drunken voice from behind the curtain. Above, attracted by the noise of the slam,* CLEA *gets out of bed, still clutching the vodka and toothmug, opens the door, and stands at the top of the stairs listening.*)

BRINDSLEY. None of this evening is happening.

CAROL. Cheer up, darling. In a few minutes everything will be all right. Mr. Bamberger will arrive in the light—he'll adore your work and give you twenty thousand pounds for your whole collection.

BRINDSLEY. (*Sarcastic.*) Oh, yes!

CAROL. Then we can buy a super Georgian house and live what's laughingly known as happily ever after. I want to leave this place just as soon as we're married.

(CLEA *hears this. Her mouth opens wide.*)

BRINDSLEY. (*Nervously.*) Sssh!

CAROL. Why? I don't want to live in a slum for our first couple of years—like other newlyweds.

BRINDSLEY. Sssh! Ssssh! . . .

CAROL. What's the matter with you?

BRINDSLEY. The gods listen, darling. They've given me a terrible night so far. They may do worse.

CAROL. (*Cooing.*) I know, darling. You've had a filthy evening. Poor babykins. But I'll fight them with you. I don't care a fig for those naughty old Goddipegs. (*Looking up.*) Do you hear? Not a single little fig!

(CLEA *aims at the voice and sends a jet of vodka splashing down over* CAROL.)

Ahh!!!

BRINDSLEY. What is it?

CAROL. It's raining!

BRINDSLEY. Don't be ridiculous.

CAROL. I'm all wet!

BRINDSLEY. How can you be?

(CLEA *throws vodka over a wider area.* HAROLD *gets it.*)

HAROLD. Hey, what's going on?

BRINDSLEY. What?

COLONEL. What the devil's the matter with you all? What are you hollerin' for? (HE *gets a slug of vodka in the face.*) Ahh!!

BRINDSLEY. (*Inspired.*) It's a leak—the water mains must have gone now.

HAROLD. Oh good God!

BRINDSLEY. It must be!

(*Mischievously,* CLEA *raps her bottle on the top stair. There is a terrified silence.* ALL *look up.*)

HAROLD. Don't say there's someone else here.

BRINDSLEY. Good Lord!

COLONEL. Who's there?

(*Silence from above.*)

Come on! I know you're there!

BRINDSLEY. (*Improvising wildly.*) I—I bet you it's Mrs. Punnet.
(CLEA *looks astonished.*)

COLONEL. Who?

BRINDSLEY. (*For* CLEA'S *benefit.*) Mrs. Punnet. My cleaning
woman.

HAROLD. Cleaning woman?

BRINDSLEY. She does for me on Mondays, Wednesdays, and Fri-
days.

CAROL. Well, what would she be doing here now?

BRINDSLEY. I've just remembered—she rang up and said she'd
look in about six to tidy up the place.

COLONEL. Dammit, man, it's almost eleven.

HAROLD. She's not that conscientious. She couldn't be!

CAROL. Not these days!

COLONEL. Well, we'll soon see. (*Calling up.*) Mrs. Punnet?

BRINDSLEY. (*Desperately.*) Don't interrupt her, sir. She doesn't
like to be disturbed when she's working. Why don't we just
leave her to potter around upstairs with her duster?

COLONEL. Let us first just see if it's her. Is that you, Mrs.
Punnet? . . .

(CLEA *keeps still.*)

COLONEL. (*Roaring.*) MRS. PUNNET!

CLEA. (*Deciding on a cockney voice of great antiquity.*) 'Allo!
Yes?

BRINDSLEY. (*Weakly.*) It is. Good heavens, Mrs. Punnet, what
on earth are you doing up there?

CLEA. I'm just giving your bedroom a bit of a tidy, sir.

BRINDSLEY. At this time of night?

(*The mischief in* CLEA *begins to take over.*)

CLEA. Better late than never, sir, as they say. I know how you
like your bedroom to be nice and inviting when you're giving one of your parties.

[107]

BRINDSLEY. Yes, yes, yes, of course . . .

COLONEL. When did you come, madam?

CLEA. Just a few minutes ago, sir. I didn't like to disturb you, so I come on up 'ere.

HAROLD. Was it you pouring all that water on us, then?

CLEA. Water? Good 'eavens, I must have upset something. It's as black as Newgate's Knocker up 'ere. Are you playing one of your saucy games, Mr. Miller?

BRINDSLEY. No, Mrs. Punnet. We've had a fuse. It's all over the house.

CLEA. Oh! A *fuse!* I thought it might be one of them saucy games in the dark, sir: Sardines or Piccadilly. The kind that end in a general squeeze-up. I know you're rather partial to kinky games, Mr. Miller, so I just wondered. (SHE *starts to come down the stairs.*)

BRINDSLEY. (*Distinctly.*) It is a fuse, Mrs. Punnet. The man's mending it now. The lights will be on *any minute!*

CLEA. Well, that'll be a relief for you, won't it? (SHE *dashes the vodka accurately in his face, passes him by and comes into the room.*)

BRINDSLEY. Yes, of course. Now why don't you just go on home?

CLEA. I'm sorry I couldn't come before, sir. I was delayed, you see. My Rosie's been taken queer again.

BRINDSLEY. I quite understand! (HE *gropes around trying to hide her, but* SHE *continuously evades him.*)

CLEA. (*Relentlessly.*) It's her tummy. There's a lump under her belly button the size of a grapefruit.

HAROLD. Oh how nasty!

CLEA. Horrid. Poor little Rosie. I said to her this evening, I said, "There's no good your being mulish, my girl. You're going to the hospital first thing tomorrow morning and getting yourself ultra-violated!"

BRINDSLEY. Well, hadn't you better be getting back to poor little Rosie! She must need you, surely?—And there's really nothing you can do here tonight.

CLEA. (*Meaningfully.*) Are you sure of that, sir?

BRINDSLEY. Positive, thank you.

(THEY *are close now.*)

CLEA. I mean, I know what this place can be like after one of your evenings. A gypsy caravan isn't in it. Gin bottles all over the floor! Bras and panties in the sink! And God knows what in the ——

(BRINDSLEY *muzzles her with his hand.* SHE *bites it hard, and* HE *drops to his knees in silent agony.*)

COLONEL. Please watch what you say, madam. You don't know it, but you're in the presence of Mr. Miller's fiancée.

CLEA. Fiancée?

COLONEL. Yes, and I am her father.

CLEA. Well, I never . . . Oh, Mr. Miller! I'm so 'appy for you! . . . Fiancée! Oh, sir! And you never told me!

BRINDSLEY. I was keeping it a surprise.

CLEA. Well, I never! Oh, how lovely! . . . May I kiss you sir, please?

BRINDSLEY. (*On his knees.*) Well yes, yes, of course . . .

(CLEA *gropes for his ear, finds it and twists it.*)

CLEA. Oh sir, I'm so pleased for you! And for *you*, Miss, too!

CAROL. Thank you.

CLEA. (*To* COLONEL MELKETT.) And for *you*, sir.

COLONEL. Thank you.

CLEA. You must be Miss Clea's father.

COLONEL. Miss Clea? I don't understand.

(*Triumphantly* SHE *sticks out her tongue at* BRINDSLEY, *who*

[109]

*collapses his length on the floor, face down, in a gesture of
total surrender. For him it is the end. The evening can hold
no further disasters for him.*)

CLEA. (*To* CAROL.) Well, I never! So you've got him at last!
Well done, Miss Clea! I never thought you would—not after
four years . . .

BRINDSLEY. No—no—no—no. . . .

CLEA. Forgive me, sir, if I'm speaking out of turn, but you
must admit four years is a long time to be courting one
woman. Four days is stretching it a bit nowadays!

BRINDSLEY. (*Weakly.*) Mrs. Punnet, *please!*

CAROL. Four years!

CLEA. Well, yes, dear. It's been all of that and a bit more really,
hasn't it? (*In a stage whisper.*) And of course it's just in
time. It was getting a bit prominent, your little bun in the
oven.

(CAROL *screeches with disgust.* BRINDSLEY *covers his ears.*)

Oh, Miss, I don't mean that's why he popped the question.
Of course it's not. He's always been stuck on you. He told
me so, not one week ago, in this room. (*Sentimentally.*)
"Mrs. Punnet," he says, "Mrs. Punnet, as far as I'm concerned you can keep the rest of them—Miss Clea will always
be on top of the heap for me." "Oh," I says, "then what
about that debutante bit, Carol, the one you're always telling me about?" "Oh, 'er," he says, "she's just a bit of
Knightsbridge candyfloss. A couple of licks and you've 'ad
'er."

(*There is a long pause.* CLEA *is now sitting on the table,
swinging her vodka bottle in absolute command of the situation.*)

COLONEL. (*Faintly; at last grappling with the situation.*) Did
you say four years, madam?

CLEA. (*In her own voice, quiet.*) Yes, Colonel. Four years, in this room.

HAROLD. I know that voice. It's Clea!

MISS FURNIVAL. (*Surprised.*) Clea!

CAROL. (*Horrified.*) Clea!

BRINDSLEY. (*Unconvincingly surprised.*) Clea!

CLEA. Surprised, Brin?

CAROL. (*Understanding.*) Clea! . . .

COLONEL. I don't understand anything that's going on in this room.

CLEA. I know. It is a very odd room, isn't it? It's like a magic dark room, where everything happens the wrong way round. Rain falls indoors, the Daily comes at night and turns in a second from a nice maid into nasty mistress.

BRINDSLEY. Be quiet, Clea!

CLEA. At last! One real word of protest! Have you finished lying, then? Have you eaten the last crumb of humble pie? Oh you coward, you bloody coward! Just because you didn't want to marry me, did you have to settle for this lot?

CAROL. Marry!

COLONEL. Marry?

CLEA. Four years of meaning to end in this triviality! Miss Laughingly Known As and her Daddipegs!

CAROL. Stop her! She's disgusting.

COLONEL. How can I, for God's sake?

CAROL. Well, where's all that bloody resource you keep talking about?

(*The* COLONEL *goes to her but takes* CLEA's *hand by mistake.*)

COLONEL. Now calm down, Dumpling. Keep your head . . . There—hold my hand, that's it, now Daddy's here. Everything is under control. All right?

CLEA. Are you sure that is your daughter's hand you're holding, Colonel?

COLONEL. What? Carol, isn't this your hand?

CAROL. No.

CLEA. You must have lived with your daughter for well over twenty years, Colonel. What remarkable use you've made of your eyes.

(*There is another pause. The* COLONEL *moves away in embarrassment.*)

CLEA. (*Wickedly.*) All right! Kinky game time! . . . Let's all play Guess the Hand.

HAROLD. Oh good God!

CLEA. Or would you rather Guess the Lips, Harold?

CAROL. How disgusting!

CLEA. Well, that's me, dear. (CAROL'*s accent.*) I'm Queen Disgustipegs!

(SHE *seizes* CAROL'*s hand and puts it into* HAROLD'*s.*) Who's that?

CAROL. I don't know.

CLEA. Guess.

CAROL. I don't know, and I don't care.

CLEA. Oh go on. Have a go!

CAROL. It's Brin, of course: You can't trick me like that! It's Brindsley's stupid hand.

HAROLD. I'm afraid you're wrong. It's me.

CAROL. (*Struggling.*) It's not. You're lying.

HAROLD. (*Holding on.*) I'm not. I don't lie.

CAROL. You're lying! . . . You're lying!

HAROLD. I'm not.

(CAROL *breaks away and blunders upstage.* SHE *is becoming hysterical.*)

CLEA. You try it, Harold. Take the hand on your right.

HAROLD. I'm not playing. It's a bloody silly game.

CLEA. Go on . . .

(SHE *seizes his hand and puts it into* BRINDSLEY'S.)

Well?

HAROLD. It's Brin.

BRINDSLEY. Yes.

CLEA. Well done! (SHE *sits on the low stool.*)

CAROL. (*Outraged.*) How does he know that? How does *he* know your hand and I don't?

BRINDSLEY. Calm down, Carol.

CAROL. Answer me! I want to know!

BRINDSLEY. Stop it!

CAROL. I won't!

BRINDSLEY. You're getting hysterical!

CAROL. Leave me alone! I want to go home.

(*And suddenly* MISS FURNIVAL *gives a sharp short scream and blunders out through the curtains.*)

MISS FURNIVAL. Prams! Prams! Prams—in the supermarket! . . .

(THEY *all freeze.* SHE *is evidently out of control in a world of her own fears.* SHE *speaks quickly and strangely.*)

All those hideous wire prams full of babies and bottles—cornflakes over there, is all they say—and then they leave you to yourself. Biscuits over there—cat food over there—fish cakes over there—Airwick over there. Pink stamps, green stamps, free balloons—television dinners—pay as you go out—oh, Daddy, it's awful! And then the Godless ones, the heathens in their leather jackets—laughing me to scorn! But, not for long. Oh, no! Who shall stand when He appeareth? He'll strike them from their motorcycles! He'll dash their helmets to the ground! Yea, verily, I say unto thee—there shall be an end of gasoline! An end to cigarette puffing and

jostling with hips . . . Keep off . . . Keep off! Keep off! . . .
(SHE *runs drunkenly across the room and collides with*
HAROLD.)

HAROLD. Come on, Ferny, I think it's time we went home.

MISS FURNIVAL. (*Pulling herself together.*) Yes. You're quite
right . . . (*With an attempt at grandeur.*) I'm sorry I can't
stay any longer, Mr. Miller; but your millionaire is unpar-
donably late. So typical of modern manners . . . Express my
regrets, if you please.

BRINDSLEY. Certainly.

(*Leaning heavily on* HAROLD's *arm* SHE *leaves the room.* HE
shuts the door after them.)

Thank you, Clea. Thank you very much.

CLEA. Any time.

BRINDSLEY. You had no right.

CLEA. No?

BRINDSLEY. *You* walked out on *me*. (HE *joins her on the low
stool.*)

CLEA. Is that what I did?

BRINDSLEY. You said you never wanted to see me again.

CLEA. I never saw you at all—how could you be walked out on?
You should live in the dark, Brindsley. It's your natural ele-
ment.

BRINDSLEY. Whatever that means.

CLEA. It means you don't really want to be seen. Why is that,
Brindsley? Do you think if someone really saw you, they
would never love you?

BRINDSLEY. Oh go away.

CLEA. I want to know.

BRINDSLEY. Yes, you always want to know. Pick-pick-pick away!
Why is *that*, Clea? Have you ever thought why you need to
do it? Well?

CLEA. Perhaps because I care about you.

BRINDSLEY. Perhaps there's nothing to care about. Just a fake artist.

CLEA. Stop pitying yourself. It's always your vice. I told you when I met you: you could either be a good artist, or a chic fake. You didn't like it, because I refused just to give you applause.

BRINDSLEY. God knows, you certainly did that!

CLEA. Is that what *she* gives you? Twenty hours of ego-massage every day?

BRINDSLEY. At least our life together isn't the replica of the Holy Inquisition you made of ours. I didn't have an affair with you: it was just four years of nooky with Torquemada!

CLEA. And don't say you didn't enjoy it!

BRINDSLEY. Enjoy it? I hated every second of it.

CLEA. Yes, I remember.

BRINDSLEY. Every second.

CLEA. I recall.

BRINDSLEY. When you left for Finland, it was the happiest day of my life.

CLEA. Mine, too!

BRINDSLEY. I sighed with relief.

CLEA. So did I.

BRINDSLEY. I went out dancing that very night.

CLEA. So did I. It was out with the lyre and the timbrel.

BRINDSLEY. Good. Then that's all right.

CLEA. Fine.

BRINDSLEY. Super!

CLEA. Duper!

BRINDSLEY. It's lovely to see you looking so happy.

CLEA. You too. Radiant with self-fulfilment.

(A *pause*.)

BRINDSLEY. If you felt like this, why did you come back?

CLEA. If *you* felt like this, why did you tell Mrs. Punnet I was still at the top of the heap?

BRINDSLEY. I never said that!

CLEA. You did.

BRINDSLEY. Never!

CLEA. You *did!*

BRINDSLEY. Of course I didn't. You invented that ten minutes ago, when you were *playing* Mrs. Punnet.

CLEA. I—Oh! So I did! . . .

(THEY *both giggle.* SHE *falls happily against his shoulder.*)

BRINDSLEY. You know something—I'm not sure she's not right. (*During this exchange the* COLONEL *and his* DAUGHTER *have been standing frozen with astonished anger. Now the outraged* FATHER *takes over.*)

COLONEL. No doubt this is very funny to you two.

CLEA. It is, quite, actually.

COLONEL. I'm not so easily amused, however, madam.

BRINDSLEY. Now look, Colonel—

COLONEL. Hold your tongue, sir, I'm talking. Do you know what would have happened to a young man in my day who dared to treat a girl the way you have treated my Dumpling?

BRINDSLEY. Well, I assume, Colonel—

COLONEL. Hold your tongue, I'm talking.

CAROL. Oh, leave it, Daddy. Let's just go home.

COLONEL. In a moment, Dumpling. Kindly leave this to me.

BRINDSLEY. Look, Carol, I can explain—

CAROL. Explain what?

BRINDSLEY. It's impossible here.

COLONEL. You understate, sir.

BRINDSLEY. Carol, you don't understand.

CAROL. What the hell's there to understand? All the time you were going with me, she was in the background—that's all

there is to it—What were you doing? Weighing us up? . . .
Here! (SHE *pulls off her engagement ring.*)

BRINDSLEY. What?

CAROL. Your ring. Take the bloody thing back!

(SHE *throws it. It hits the* COLONEL *in the eye.*)

COLONEL. My eye! My damned eye!

(CLEA *starts to laugh again.*
In mounting fury, clutching his eye.)

Oh very droll, madam! Very droll indeed! Laugh your fill!
Miller! I asked you a question. Do you know what would
have happened to a young lout like you in my day?

BRINDSLEY. Happened, sir?

COLONEL. (*Quietly.*) You'd have been thrashed, sir.

BRINDSLEY. (*Nervous.*) Thrashed—

(*The* MAN OF WAR *begins to go after him, feeling his way in
the dark—like some furious robot.*)

COLONEL. You'd have felt the mark of a father's horsewhip
across your seducer's shoulders. You'd have gone down on
your cad's bended knees, and begged my daughter's pardon
for the insults you've offered her tonight.

BRINDSLEY. (*Retreating before the* COLONEL's *groping advance.*)
Would I, sir?

COLONEL. You'd have raised your guttersnipe voice in a piteous
scream for mercy and forgiveness!

(*A terrible scream is heard from the hall.* THEY *freeze, listening as it comes nearer and nearer, then the door is flung open
and* HAROLD *plunges into the room.* HE *is wild-eyed with rage:
a lit and bent taper shakes in his furious hand.*)

HAROLD. Ooooooh! You villain!

BRINDSLEY. Harold—

HAROLD. You skunky, conniving little villain!

BRINDSLEY. What's the matter?

HAROLD. (*Raging.*) Have you seen the state of my room? My room? My lovely room, the most elegant and cared for in this entire district?—one chair turned absolutely upside down, one chair on top of another like a Portobello junkshop! And that's not all, is it, Brindsley? Oh no, that's not the worst by a long chalk, is it, Brindsley?

BRINDSLEY. Long chalk?

HAROLD. Don't play the innocent with me. I thought I had a friend living all these years. I didn't know I was living opposite a Light-fingered Lenny!

BRINDSLEY. Harold!—

HAROLD. (*Hysterical.*) This is my reward, isn't it?—After years of looking after you, sweeping and tidying up this place, because you're too much of a slut to do it for yourself—to have my best pieces stolen from me to impress your new girl friend and her daddy. Or did she help you?

BRINDSLEY. Harold, it was an emergency.

HAROLD. Don't talk to me: I don't want to know! I know what you think of me now . . . "Don't tell Harold about the engagement. He's not to be trusted. He's not a friend. He's just someone to steal things from!"

BRINDSLEY. You know that's not true.

HAROLD. (*Shrieking—in one hysterical breath.*) I know I was the last one to know—that's what I know! I have to find it out in a room full of strangers. Me, who's listened to more of your miseries in the small hours of the morning than anyone else would put up with! All your boring talk about women, hour after hour, as if no one's got troubles but you!—

CLEA. She's getting hysterical, dear. Ignore her.

HAROLD. It's you who's going to be ignored, Clea. (*To* BRINDS-

LEY.) As for you, all I can say about your engagement is this: you deserve each other, you and that little nit.

(CAROL *gives a shriek.*)

BRINDSLEY. Carol!

HAROLD. Oh, so you're there, are you?—Skulking in the shadows!

BRINDSLEY. Leave her alone!

HAROLD. I'm not going to touch her. I just want my things and I'll be off. Did you hear me, Brindsley? You give me my things now, or I'll call the police.

BRINDSLEY. Don't be ridiculous.

HAROLD. (*Grimly.*) Item: One lyre-back Regency chair, in lacquered mahogany with Ormolu inlay and appliqué work on the cushions.

BRINDSLEY. In front of you. (HE *thrusts the taper at it.*)

HAROLD. Ta. Item: One half-back sofa—likewise Regency—supported by claw legs and upholstered in a rich silk of bottle green to match the aforesaid chair.

BRINDSLEY. In the studio.

HAROLD. Unbelievable! Item: One Coalport vase, dated 1809, decorated on the rim with a pleasing design of daisies and peonies.

BRINDSLEY. On the floor.

HAROLD. Ta.

(BRINDSLEY *hands it to him.*)

Ooooh! You've even taken the flowers! I'll come back for the chair and sofa in a minute. (*Drawing himself up with all the offended dignity of which a* HAROLD GORRINGE *is capable.*) This is the end of our relationship, Brindsley. We won't be speaking again, I don't think.

(HE *twitches his raincoat off the table. Inside it, of course, is the Buddha, which falls on the floor and smashes beyond repair. There is a terrible silence. Trying to keep his voice under control:*)

Do you know what that statue was worth? Do you? More money than you'll ever see in your whole life, even if you sell every piece of that nasty, rusty rubbish. (*With the quietness of the mad.*) I think I'm going to have to smash you, Brindsley.

BRINDSLEY. (*Nervously.*) Now steady on, Harold . . . don't be rash . . .

HAROLD. Yes, I'm very much afraid I'll have to smash you . . . Smash for smash—that's fair do's. (HE *pulls one of the long metal prongs out of the sculpture.*) Smash for smash. Smash for *smash!*

(*Insanely* HE *advances on* BRINDSLEY *holding the prong like a sword, the taper burning in his other hand.*)

BRINDSLEY. (*Retreating.*) Stop it, Harold. You've gone mad!

COLONEL. Well done, sir. I think it's time for the reckoning.

(*The* COLONEL *grabs the other prong and also advances.*)

BRINDSLEY. (*Retreating from them* BOTH.) Now just a minute, Colonel. Be reasonable! . . . Let's not revert to savages! . . . Harold, I appeal to you—you've always had civilized instincts! Don't join the Army! . . .

CAROL. (*Grimly advancing also.*) Get him, Daddy! Get him! Get him!

BRINDSLEY. (*Horrified at her.*) Carol!

CAROL. (*Malevolently.*) Get him! Get him! Get him! Get . . .

BRINDSLEY. Clea!

(CLEA *leaps up and blows out the taper. Lights up.*)

COLONEL. Dammit!

(CLEA *grabs* BRINDSLEY'S *hand and pulls him out of danger. To* CLEA.)

Careful, my little Dumpling. Keep out of the way.

HAROLD. (*To* CAROL.) Hush up, Colonel. We'll be able to hear them breathing.

COLONEL. Clever idea! Smart tactics, sir!

(*Silence.* THEY *listen.* BRINDSLEY *climbs carefully onto the table and silently pulls* CLEA *up after him.* HAROLD *and the* COLONEL, *prodding and slashing the darkness with their swords, grimly hunt their quarry. Twenty seconds. Suddenly, with a bang* SCHUPPANZIGH *opens the trap from below.* BOTH MEN *advance on it warily. The* ELECTRICIAN *disappears again below.* THEY *have almost reached it, on tiptoe, when there is another crash—this time from the hall.* SOMEONE *has again tripped over the milk bottles.* HAROLD *and the* COLONEL *immediately swing round and start stalking upstage, still on tiptoe.*

Enter GEORG BAMBERGER. HE *is quite evidently a millionaire. Dressed in the Gulbenkian manner,* HE *wears a beard, an eyeglass, a frock coat, a top hat and an orchid.* HE *carries a large deaf aid.*

Bewildered, HE *advances into the room. Stealthily, the* TWO *armed* MEN *stalk him upstage as* HE *silently gropes his way downstage and passes between them.*)

BAMBERGER. (*Speaking in a middle-aged German voice, as near to the voice of* SCHUPPANZIGH *as possible.*) Hallo, please! Mr. Miller?

(HAROLD *and the* COLONEL *spin round in a third direction.*)

HAROLD. Oh, it's the electrician!

BAMBERGER. Hallo, please?

COLONEL. What the devil are you doing up here?

(SCHUPPANZIGH *appears at the trap.*)

Have you mended the fuse?

HAROLD. Or are you going to keep us in the dark all night?

SCHUPPANZIGH. Don't worry. The fuse is mended.

(HE *comes out of the trap.*

BAMBERGER *goes round the stage, right.*)

HAROLD. Thank God for that.

BAMBERGER. (*Still groping around.*) Hallo, please? Mr. Miller— vere are you? Vy zis darkness? Is a joke, yes?

SCHUPPANZIGH. (*Incensed.*) Ah, no! That is not very funny, good people—just because I am a foreigner, to imitate my voice. You English can be the rudest people on earth!

BAMBERGER. (*Imperiously.*) Mr. Miller! I have come here to give attention to your sculptures!

SCHUPPANZIGH. *Gott in himmel!*

BAMBERGER. *Gott in himmel!*

BRINDSLEY. God, it's him! Bamberger!

CLEA. He's come!

HAROLD. Bamberger!

COLONEL. Bamberger!

(THEY *freeze. The* MILLIONAIRE *sets off, left, toward the open trap.*)

BRINDSLEY. Don't worry, Mr. Bamberger. We've had a fuse, but it's mended now.

BAMBERGER. (*Irritably.*) Mr. Miller!

CLEA. You'll have to speak up. He's deaf.

BRINDSLEY. (*Shouting.*) Don't worry, Mr. Bamberger! We've had a fuse, but it's all right now! . . .

(*Standing on the table,* HE *clasps* CLEA *happily.* BAMBERGER *misses the trap by inches.*)

Oh, Clea, that's true. Everything's all right now! Just in the nick of time!

(*But as* HE *says this* BAMBERGER *turns and falls into the open trap door.* SCHUPPANZIGH *slams it to with his foot.*)

SCHUPPANZIGH. So! Here's now an end to your troubles! Like